This book belongs to

_____

LUTHER'S SMALL CATECHISM

with Explanation

LUTHER'S SMALL CATECHISM

with Explanation

CONCORDIA PUBLISHING HOUSE • SAINT LOUIS

This publication may be available in braille, in large print, or on cassette tape for the visually impaired. Please allow 8 to 12 weeks for delivery. Write to Lutheran Blind Mission, 7550 Watson Rd., St. Louis, MO 63119-4409; call toll-free 1-888-215-2455; or visit the Web site: www.blindmission.org.

Manufactured in the United States of America

CIP data can be found on page 296.

3 4 5 6 7 8 9 10   14 13 12 11 10 09 08 07

CONTENTS

Luther's Small Catechism

LUTHER'S
SMALL
CATECHISM

Section 1

THE TEN COMMANDMENTS

**As the head of the family should teach them
in a simple way to his household**

The First Commandment

You shall have no other gods.

What does this mean? We should fear, love, and trust in God above all things.

The Second Commandment

You shall not misuse the name of the Lord your God.

What does this mean? We should fear and love God so that we do not curse, swear, use satanic arts, lie, or deceive by His name, but call upon it in every trouble, pray, praise, and give thanks.

The Third Commandment
Remember the Sabbath day by keeping it holy.

What does this mean? We should fear and love God so that we do not despise preaching and His Word, but hold it sacred and gladly hear and learn it.

The Fourth Commandment
Honor your father and your mother.

What does this mean? We should fear and love God so that we do not despise or anger our parents and other authorities, but honor them, serve and obey them, love and cherish them.

The Fifth Commandment
You shall not murder.

What does this mean? We should fear and love God so that we do not hurt or harm our neighbor in his body, but help and support him in every physical need.

The Sixth Commandment
You shall not commit adultery.

What does this mean? We should fear and love God so that we lead a sexually pure and decent life in what we say and do, and husband and wife love and honor each other.

The Seventh Commandment
You shall not steal.

What does this mean? We should fear and love God so that we do not take our neighbor's money or possessions, or get them in any dishonest way, but help him to improve and protect his possessions and income.

The Eighth Commandment
You shall not give false testimony against your neighbor.

What does this mean? We should fear and love God so that we do not tell lies about our neighbor, betray him, slander him, or hurt his reputation, but defend him, speak well of him, and explain everything in the kindest way.

The Ninth Commandment
You shall not covet your neighbor's house.

What does this mean? We should fear and love God so that we do not scheme to get our neighbor's inheritance or house, or get it in a way which only appears right, but help and be of service to him in keeping it.

The Tenth Commandment
You shall not covet your neighbor's wife, or his manservant or maidservant, his ox or donkey, or anything that belongs to your neighbor.

What does this mean? We should fear and love God so that we do not entice or force away our neighbor's wife, workers, or animals, or turn them against him, but urge them to stay and do their duty.

[The text of the commandments is from **Ex. 20:3, 7, 8, 12–17.**]

The Close of the Commandments

What does God say about all these commandments?

He says, "I, the Lord your God, am a jealous God, punishing the children for the sin of the fathers to the third and fourth generation of those who hate Me, but showing love to a thousand generations of those who love Me and keep My commandments." (Ex. 20: 5–6)

What does this mean? God threatens to punish all who break these commandments. Therefore, we should fear His wrath and not do anything against them. But He promises grace and every blessing to all who keep these commandments. Therefore, we should also love and trust in Him and gladly do what He commands.

THE CREED

As the head of the family should teach it in a simple way to his household

The First Article
Creation

I believe in God, the Father Almighty, Maker of heaven and earth.

What does this mean? I believe that God has made me and all creatures; that He has given me my body and soul, eyes, ears, and all my members, my reason and all my senses, and still takes care of them.

He also gives me clothing and shoes, food and drink, house and home, wife and children, land, animals, and all I have. He richly and daily provides me with all that I need to support this body and life.

He defends me against all danger and guards and protects me from all evil.

All this He does only out of fatherly, divine goodness and mercy, without any merit or worthiness in me. For all this it is my duty to thank and praise, serve and obey Him.

This is most certainly true.

The Second Article
Redemption

And in Jesus Christ, His only Son, our Lord, who was conceived by the Holy Spirit, born of the Virgin Mary, suffered under Pontius Pilate, was crucified, died and was buried. He descended into hell. The third day He rose again from the dead. He ascended into heaven and sits at the right hand of God, the Father Almighty. From thence He will come to judge the living and the dead.

What does this mean? I believe that Jesus Christ, true God, begotten of the Father from eternity, and also true man, born of the Virgin Mary, is my Lord,

who has redeemed me, a lost and condemned person, purchased and won me from all sins, from death, and from the power of the devil; not with gold or silver, but with His holy, precious blood and with His innocent suffering and death,

that I may be His own and live under Him in His kingdom and serve Him in everlasting righteousness, innocence, and blessedness, just as He is risen from the dead, lives and reigns to all eternity.

This is most certainly true.

The Third Article
Sanctification

I believe in the Holy Spirit, the holy Christian church, the communion of saints, the forgiveness of sins, the resurrection of the body, and the life everlasting. Amen.

What does this mean? I believe that I cannot by my own reason or strength believe in Jesus Christ, my Lord, or come to Him; but the Holy Spirit has called me by the Gospel, enlightened me with His gifts, sanctified and kept me in the true faith.

In the same way He calls, gathers, enlightens, and sanctifies the whole Christian church on earth, and keeps it with Jesus Christ in the one true faith.

In this Christian church He daily and richly forgives all my sins and the sins of all believers.

On the Last Day He will raise me and all the dead, and give eternal life to me and all believers in Christ.

This is most certainly true.

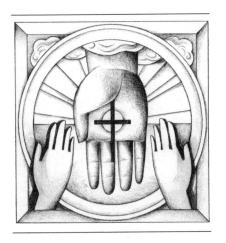

THE LORD'S PRAYER

**As the head of the family should teach it
in a simple way to his household**

Our Father who art in heaven, hallowed be Thy name, Thy kingdom come, Thy will be done on earth as it is in heaven. Give us this day our daily bread; and forgive us our trespasses as we forgive those who trespass against us; and lead us not into temptation, but deliver us from evil. For Thine is the kingdom and the power and the glory forever and ever. Amen.

Our Father in heaven, hallowed be Your name, Your kingdom come, Your will be done on earth as in heaven. Give us today our daily bread. Forgive us our sins as we forgive those who sin against us. Lead us not into temptation, but deliver us from evil. For the kingdom, the power, and the glory are Yours now and forever. Amen.

The Introduction
Our Father who art in heaven.
Our Father in heaven.

What does this mean? With these words God tenderly invites us to believe that He is our true Father and that we are His true children, so that with all boldness and confidence we may ask Him as dear children ask their dear father.

The First Petition
Hallowed be Thy name.
Hallowed be Your name.

What does this mean? God's name is certainly holy in itself, but we pray in this petition that it may be kept holy among us also.

How is God's name kept holy? God's name is kept holy when the Word of God is taught in its truth and purity, and we, as the children of God, also lead holy lives according to it. Help us to do this, dear Father in heaven! But anyone who teaches or lives contrary to God's Word profanes the name of God among us. Protect us from this, heavenly Father!

The Second Petition
Thy kingdom come.
Your kingdom come.

What does this mean? The kingdom of God certainly comes by itself without our prayer, but we pray in this petition that it may come to us also.

How does God's kingdom come? God's kingdom comes when our heavenly Father gives us His Holy Spirit, so that by His grace we believe His holy Word and lead godly lives here in time and there in eternity.

The Third Petition

Thy will be done on earth as it is in heaven.

Your will be done on earth as in heaven.

What does this mean? The good and gracious will of God is done even without our prayer, but we pray in this petition that it may be done among us also.

How is God's will done? God's will is done

when He breaks and hinders every evil plan and purpose of the devil, the world, and our sinful nature, which do not want us to hallow God's name or let His kingdom come;

and when He strengthens and keeps us firm in His Word and faith until we die.

This is His good and gracious will.

The Fourth Petition

Give us this day our daily bread.

Give us today our daily bread.

What does this mean? God certainly gives daily bread to everyone without our prayers, even to all evil people, but we pray in this petition that God would lead us to realize this and to receive our daily bread with thanksgiving.

What is meant by daily bread? Daily bread includes

everything that has to do with the support and needs of the body, such as food, drink, clothing, shoes, house, home, land, animals, money, goods, a devout husband or wife, devout children, devout workers, devout and faithful rulers, good government, good weather, peace, health, self-control, good reputation, good friends, faithful neighbors, and the like.

The Fifth Petition

**And forgive us our trespasses
as we forgive those who trespass against us.**

*Forgive us our sins
as we forgive those who sin against us.*

What does this mean? We pray in this petition that our Father in heaven would not look at our sins, or deny our prayer because of them. We are neither worthy of the things for which we pray, nor have we deserved them, but we ask that He would give them all to us by grace, for we daily sin much and surely deserve nothing but punishment. So we too will sincerely forgive and gladly do good to those who sin against us.

The Sixth Petition

And lead us not into temptation.

Lead us not into temptation.

What does this mean? God tempts no one. We pray in this petition that God would guard and keep us so that the devil, the world, and our sinful nature may not deceive us or mislead us into false belief, despair, and other great shame and vice. Although we are attacked by these things, we pray that we may finally overcome them and win the victory.

The Seventh Petition

But deliver us from evil.
But deliver us from evil.

What does this mean? We pray in this petition, in summary, that our Father in heaven would rescue us from every evil of body and soul, possessions and reputation, and finally, when our last hour comes, give us a blessed end, and graciously take us from this valley of sorrow to Himself in heaven.

The Conclusion

For Thine is the kingdom and the power and the glory forever and ever.* Amen.
For the kingdom,
the power, and the glory are Yours
now and forever. Amen.*

What does this mean? This means that I should be certain that these petitions are pleasing to our Father in heaven, and are heard by Him; for He Himself has commanded us to pray in this way and has promised to hear us. Amen, amen means "yes, yes, it shall be so."

*These words were not in Luther's Small Catechism.

THE SACRAMENT
OF HOLY BAPTISM

**As the head of the family should teach it
in a simple way to his household**

First
What is Baptism?

Baptism is not just plain water, but it is the water included in God's command and combined with God's word.

Which is that word of God?

Christ our Lord says in the last chapter of Matthew: "Therefore go and make disciples of all nations, baptizing them in the name of the Father and of the Son and of the Holy Spirit." **(Matt. 28:19)**

Second

What benefits does Baptism give?

It works forgiveness of sins, rescues from death and the devil, and gives eternal salvation to all who believe this, as the words and promises of God declare.

Which are these words and promises of God?

Christ our Lord says in the last chapter of Mark: "Whoever believes and is baptized will be saved, but whoever does not believe will be condemned." **(Mark 16:16)**

Third

How can water do such great things?

Certainly not just water, but the word of God in and with the water does these things, along with the faith which trusts this word of God in the water. For without God's word the water is plain water and no Baptism. But with the word of God it is a Baptism, that is, a life-giving water, rich in grace, and a washing of the new birth in the Holy Spirit, as St. Paul says in Titus, chapter three:

"He saved us through the washing of rebirth and renewal by the Holy Spirit, whom He poured out on us generously through Jesus Christ our Savior, so that, having been justified by His grace, we might become heirs having the hope of eternal life. This is a trustworthy saying." **(Titus 3:5–8)**

Fourth

What does such baptizing with water indicate?

It indicates that the Old Adam in us should by daily contrition and repentance be drowned and die with all sins and evil desires, and that a new man should daily emerge and arise to live before God in righteousness and purity forever.

Where is this written?

St. Paul writes in Romans chapter six: "We were therefore buried with Him through baptism into death in order that, just as Christ was raised from the dead through the glory of the Father, we too may live a new life." **(Rom. 6:4)**

CONFESSION

How Christians should be taught to confess

What is Confession?

Confession has two parts.

First, that we confess our sins, and

second, that we receive absolution, that is, forgiveness, from the pastor as from God Himself, not doubting, but firmly believing that by it our sins are forgiven before God in heaven.

What sins should we confess?

Before God we should plead guilty of all sins, even those we are not aware of, as we do in the Lord's Prayer; but before the pastor we should confess only those sins which we know and feel in our hearts.

Which are these?

Consider your place in life according to the Ten
Commandments: Are you a father, mother, son,
daughter, husband, wife, or worker? Have you been
disobedient, unfaithful, or lazy? Have you been hot-
tempered, rude, or quarrelsome? Have you hurt
someone by your words or deeds? Have you stolen,
been negligent, wasted anything, or done any harm?

A SHORT FORM OF CONFESSION

[Luther intended the following form to serve only as an example of private
confession for Christians of his time. For a contemporary form of individual
confession, see *Lutheran Worship*, pp. 310–11.]

The penitent says:

Dear confessor, I ask you please to hear my confession and to pronounce forgiveness in order to fulfill
God's will.

I, a poor sinner, plead guilty before God of all sins. In
particular I confess before you that as a servant, maid,
etc., I, sad to say, serve my master unfaithfully, for in this
and that I have not done what I was told to do. I have
made him angry and caused him to curse. I have been
negligent and allowed damage to be done. I have also
been offensive in words and deeds. I have quarreled with
my peers. I have grumbled about the lady of the house
and cursed her. I am sorry for all of this and I ask for
grace. I want to do better.

A master or lady of the house may say:

In particular I confess before you that I have not
faithfully guided my children, servants, and wife to the

glory of God. I have cursed. I have set a bad example by
indecent words and deeds. I have hurt my neighbor and
spoken evil of him. I have overcharged, sold inferior
merchandise, and given less than was paid for.

[Let the penitent confess whatever else he has done
against God's commandments and his own position.]

If, however, someone does not find himself burdened
with these or greater sins, he should not trouble himself
or search for or invent other sins, and thereby make
confession a torture. Instead, he should mention one or
two that he knows: In particular I confess that I have
cursed; I have used improper words; I have neglected
this or that, etc. Let that be enough.

But if you know of none at all (which hardly seems
possible), then mention none in particular, but receive
the forgiveness upon the general confession which you
make to God before the confessor.

Then the confessor shall say:

God be merciful to you and strengthen your faith.
Amen.

Furthermore:

Do you believe that my forgiveness is God's forgiveness?

Yes, dear confessor.

Then let him say:

Let it be done for you as you believe. And I, by the
command of our Lord Jesus Christ, forgive you your
sins in the name of the Father and of the Son and of the
Holy Spirit. Amen. Go in peace.

A confessor will know additional passages with which to comfort and to strengthen the faith of those who have great burdens of conscience or are sorrowful and distressed.

This is intended only as a general form of confession.

What is the Office of the Keys?*

The Office of the Keys is that special authority which Christ has given to His church on earth to forgive the sins of repentant sinners, but to withhold forgiveness from the unrepentant as long as they do not repent.

Where is this written?*

This is what St. John the Evangelist writes in chapter twenty: The Lord Jesus breathed on His disciples and said, "Receive the Holy Spirit. If you forgive anyone his sins, they are forgiven; if you do not forgive them, they are not forgiven." **(John 20:22–23)**

What do you believe
according to these words?*

I believe that when the called ministers of Christ deal with us by His divine command, in particular when they exclude openly unrepentant sinners from the Christian congregation and absolve those who repent of their sins and want to do better, this is just as valid and certain, even in heaven, as if Christ our dear Lord dealt with us Himself.

*This question may not have been composed by Luther himself but reflects his teaching and was included in editions of the catechism during his lifetime.

THE SACRAMENT
OF THE ALTAR

**As the head of the family should teach it
in a simple way to his household**

What is the Sacrament of the Altar?

It is the true body and blood of our Lord Jesus Christ under the bread and wine, instituted by Christ Himself for us Christians to eat and to drink.

Where is this written?

The holy Evangelists Matthew, Mark, Luke, and St. Paul write:

Our Lord Jesus Christ, on the night when He was betrayed, took bread, and when He had given thanks, He broke it and gave it to the disciples and said: "Take, eat; this is My body, which is given for you. This do in remembrance of Me."

In the same way also He took the cup after supper, and when He had given thanks, He gave it to them, saying, "Drink of it, all of you; this cup is the new testament in My blood, which is shed for you for the forgiveness of sins. This do, as often as you drink it, in remembrance of Me."

What is the benefit of this eating and drinking?

These words, "Given and shed for you for the forgiveness of sins," show us that in the Sacrament forgiveness of sins, life, and salvation are given us through these words. For where there is forgiveness of sins, there is also life and salvation.

How can bodily eating and drinking do such great things?

Certainly not just eating and drinking do these things, but the words written here: "Given and shed for you for the forgiveness of sins." These words, along with the bodily eating and drinking, are the main thing in the Sacrament. Whoever believes these words has exactly what they say: "forgiveness of sins."

Who receives this sacrament worthily?

Fasting and bodily preparation are certainly fine outward training. But that person is truly worthy and well prepared who has faith in these words: "Given and shed for you for the forgiveness of sins."

But anyone who does not believe these words or doubts them is unworthy and unprepared, for the words "for you" require all hearts to believe.

Section 2

DAILY PRAYERS

**How the head of the family should teach his household
to pray morning and evening**

Morning Prayer

*In the morning when you get up, make the sign of the
holy cross and say:*

In the name of the Father and of the ✠ Son and of the
Holy Spirit. Amen.

*Then, kneeling or standing, repeat the Creed and the
Lord's Prayer. If you choose, you may also say this little
prayer:*

I thank You, my heavenly Father, through Jesus Christ, Your dear Son, that You have kept me this night from all harm and danger; and I pray that You would keep me this day also from sin and every evil, that all my doings and life may please You. For into Your hands I commend myself, my body and soul, and all things. Let Your holy angel be with me, that the evil foe may have no power over me. Amen.

Then go joyfully to your work, singing a hymn, like that of the Ten Commandments, or whatever your devotion may suggest.

Evening Prayer

In the evening when you go to bed, make the sign of the holy cross and say:

In the name of the Father and of the ✠ Son and of the Holy Spirit. Amen.

Then kneeling or standing, repeat the Creed and the Lord's Prayer. If you choose, you may also say this little prayer:

I thank You, my heavenly Father, through Jesus Christ, Your dear Son, that You have graciously kept me this day; and I pray that You would forgive me all my sins where I have done wrong, and graciously keep me this night. For into Your hands I commend myself, my body and soul, and all things. Let Your holy angel be with me, that the evil foe may have no power over me. Amen.

Then go to sleep at once and in good cheer.

**How the head of the family should teach his household
to ask a blessing and return thanks**

Asking a Blessing

*The children and members of the household shall go to
the table reverently, fold their hands, and say:*

The eyes of all look to You, [O Lord,] and You give
them their food at the proper time. You open Your hand
and satisfy the desires of every living thing. **(Ps. 145:
15–16)**

Then shall be said the Lord's Prayer and the following:

Lord God, heavenly Father, bless us and these Your
gifts which we receive from Your bountiful goodness,
through Jesus Christ, our Lord. Amen.

Returning Thanks

*Also, after eating, they shall, in like manner, reverently
and with folded hands say:*

Give thanks to the Lord, for He is good. His love
endures forever. [He] gives food to every creature. He
provides food for the cattle and for the young ravens
when they call. His pleasure is not in the strength of the
horse, nor His delight in the legs of a man; the Lord
delights in those who fear Him, who put their hope in
His unfailing love. **(Ps. 136:1, 25; 147:9–11)**

Then shall be said the Lord's Prayer and the following:

We thank You, Lord God, heavenly Father, for all Your
benefits, through Jesus Christ, our Lord, who lives and
reigns with You and the Holy Spirit forever and ever.
Amen.

Section 3

TABLE OF DUTIES

Certain passages of Scripture for various holy orders and positions, admonishing them about their duties and responsibilities

To Bishops, Pastors, and Preachers

The overseer must be above reproach, the husband of but one wife, temperate, self-controlled, respectable, hospitable, able to teach, not given to drunkenness, not violent but gentle, not quarrelsome, not a lover of money. He must manage his own family well and see that his children obey him with proper respect. **1 Tim. 3:2–4**

He must not be a recent convert, or he may become conceited and fall under the same judgment as the devil. **1 Tim. 3:6**

He must hold firmly to the trustworthy message as it has been taught, so that he can encourage others by sound doctrine and refute those who oppose it. **Titus 1:9**

What the Hearers Owe Their Pastors

The Lord has commanded that those who preach the gospel should receive their living from the gospel. **1 Cor. 9:14**

Anyone who receives instruction in the word must share all good things with his instructor. Do not be deceived: God cannot be mocked. A man reaps what he sows. **Gal. 6:6–7**

The elders who direct the affairs of the church well are worthy of double honor, especially those whose work is preaching and teaching. For the Scripture says, "Do not muzzle the ox while it is treading out the grain," and "The worker deserves his wages." **1 Tim. 5:17–18**

We ask you, brothers, to respect those who work hard among you, who are over you in the Lord and who admonish you. Hold them in the highest regard in love because of their work. Live in peace with each other. **1 Thess. 5:12–13**

Obey your leaders and submit to their authority. They keep watch over you as men who must give an account. Obey them so that their work will be a joy, not a burden, for that would be of no advantage to you. **Heb. 13:17**

Of Civil Government

Everyone must submit himself to the governing authorities, for there is no authority except that which

God has established. The authorities that exist have been established by God. Consequently, he who rebels against the authority is rebelling against what God has instituted, and those who do so will bring judgment on themselves. For rulers hold no terror for those who do right, but for those who do wrong. Do you want to be free from fear of the one in authority? Then do what is right and he will commend you. For he is God's servant to do you good. But if you do wrong, be afraid, for he does not bear the sword for nothing. He is God's servant, an agent of wrath to bring punishment on the wrongdoer. **Rom. 13:1–4**

Of Citizens

Give to Caesar what is Caesar's, and to God what is God's. **Matt. 22:21**

It is necessary to submit to the authorities, not only because of possible punishment but also because of conscience. This is also why you pay taxes, for the authorities are God's servants, who give their full time to governing. Give everyone what you owe him: If you owe taxes, pay taxes; if revenue, then revenue; if respect, then respect; if honor, then honor. **Rom. 13:5–7**

I urge, then, first of all, that requests, prayers, intercession and thanksgiving be made for everyone—for kings and all those in authority, that we may live peaceful and quiet lives in all godliness and holiness. This is good, and pleases God our Savior. **1 Tim. 2:1–3**

Remind the people to be subject to rulers and authorities, to be obedient, to be ready to do whatever is good. **Titus 3:1**

Submit yourselves for the Lord's sake to every authority instituted among men: whether to the king, as the supreme authority, or to governors, who are sent by him to punish those who do wrong and to commend those who do right. **1 Peter 2:13–14**

To Husbands

Husbands, in the same way be considerate as you live with your wives, and treat them with respect as the weaker partner and as heirs with you of the gracious gift of life, so that nothing will hinder your prayers. **1 Peter 3:7**

Husbands, love your wives and do not be harsh with them. **Col. 3:19**

To Wives

Wives, submit to your husbands as to the Lord. **Eph. 5:22**

They were submissive to their own husbands, like Sarah, who obeyed Abraham and called him her master. You are her daughters if you do what is right and do not give way to fear. **1 Peter 3:5–6**

To Parents

Fathers, do not exasperate your children; instead, bring them up in the training and instruction of the Lord. **Eph. 6:4**

To Children

Children, obey your parents in the Lord, for this is right. "Honor your father and your mother"—which is the first commandment with a promise—"that it may go well with you and that you may enjoy long life on the earth." **Eph. 6:1–3**

To Workers of All Kinds

Slaves, obey your earthly masters with respect and fear, and with sincerity of heart, just as you would obey

Christ. Obey them not only to win their favor when their eye is on you, but like slaves of Christ, doing the will of God from your heart. Serve wholeheartedly, as if you were serving the Lord, not men, because you know that the Lord will reward everyone for whatever good he does, whether he is slave or free. **Eph. 6:5–8**

To Employers and Supervisors

Masters, treat your slaves in the same way. Do not threaten them, since you know that He who is both their Master and yours is in heaven, and there is no favoritism with Him. **Eph. 6:9**

To Youth

Young men, in the same way be submissive to those who are older. All of you, clothe yourselves with humility toward one another, because, "God opposes the proud but gives grace to the humble." Humble yourselves, therefore, under God's mighty hand, that He may lift you up in due time. **1 Peter 5:5–6**

To Widows

The widow who is really in need and left all alone puts her hope in God and continues night and day to pray and to ask God for help. But the widow who lives for pleasure is dead even while she lives. **1 Tim. 5:5–6**

To Everyone

The commandments . . . are summed up in this one rule: "Love your neighbor as yourself." **Rom. 13:9**

I urge . . . that requests, prayers, intercession and thanksgiving be made for everyone. **1 Tim. 2:1**

Let each his lesson learn with care,
and all the household well shall fare.

Section 4

CHRISTIAN QUESTIONS WITH THEIR ANSWERS*

Prepared by Dr. Martin Luther for those who intend to go to the Sacrament

After confession and instruction in the Ten Commandments, the Creed, the Lord's Prayer, and the Sacraments of Baptism and the Lord's Supper, the pastor may ask, or Christians may ask themselves these questions:

1. Do you believe that you are a sinner?

Yes, I believe it. I am a sinner.

* The "Christian Questions with Their Answers," designating Luther as the author, first appeared in an edition of the Small Catechism in 1551.

2. How do you know this?
From the Ten Commandments, which I have not
kept.

3. Are you sorry for your sins?
Yes, I am sorry that I have sinned against God.

4. What have you deserved from God because of your
sins?
His wrath and displeasure, temporal death, and
eternal damnation. See **Rom. 6:21, 23.**

5. Do you hope to be saved?
Yes, that is my hope.

6. In whom then do you trust?
In my dear Lord Jesus Christ.

7. Who is Christ?
The Son of God, true God and man.

8. How many Gods are there?
Only one, but there are three persons: Father, Son,
and Holy Spirit.

9. What has Christ done for you that you trust in Him?
He died for me and shed His blood for me on the
cross for the forgiveness of sins.

10. Did the Father also die for you?
He did not. The Father is God only, as is the Holy
Spirit; but the Son is both true God and true man.
He died for me and shed His blood for me.

11. How do you know this?
From the holy Gospel, from the words instituting
the Sacrament, and by His body and blood given me
as a pledge in the Sacrament.

12. What are the words of institution?
    Our Lord Jesus Christ, on the night when He was betrayed, took bread, and when He had given thanks, He broke it and gave it to the disciples and said: "Take eat; this is My body, which is given for you. This do in remembrance of Me."
    In the same way also He took the cup after supper, and when He had given thanks, He gave it to them, saying: "Drink of it, all of you; this cup is the new testament in My blood, which is shed for you for the forgiveness of sins. This do, as often as you drink it, in remembrance of Me."

13. Do you believe, then, that the true body and blood of Christ are in the Sacrament?
    Yes, I believe it.

14. What convinces you to believe this?
    The word of Christ: Take, eat, this is My body; drink of it, all of you, this is My blood.

15. What should we do when we eat His body and drink His blood, and in this way receive His pledge?
    We should remember and proclaim His death and the shedding of His blood, as He taught us: This do, as often as you drink it, in remembrance of Me.

16. Why should we remember and proclaim His death?
    First, so that we may learn to believe that no creature could make satisfaction for our sins. Only Christ, true God and man, could do that. Second, so we may learn to be horrified by our sins, and to regard them as very serious. Third, so we may find joy and comfort in Christ alone, and through faith in Him be saved.

17. What motivated Christ to die and make full payment for your sins?
His great love for His Father and for me and other sinners, as it is written in **John 14; Romans 5; Galatians 2;** and **Ephesians 5.**

18. Finally, why do you wish to go to the Sacrament?
That I may learn to believe that Christ, out of great love, died for my sin, and also learn from Him to love God and my neighbor.

19. What should admonish and encourage a Christian to receive the Sacrament frequently?
First, both the command and the promise of Christ the Lord. Second, his own pressing need, because of which the command, encouragement, and promise are given.

20. But what should you do if you are not aware of this need and have no hunger and thirst for the Sacrament?
To such a person no better advice can be given than this: first, he should touch his body to see if he still has flesh and blood. Then he should believe what the Scriptures say of it in **Galatians 5** and **Romans 7.** Second, he should look around to see whether he is still in the world, and remember that there will be no lack of sin and trouble, as the Scriptures say in **John 15–16** and in **1 John 2** and **5.**
Third, he will certainly have the devil also around him, who with his lying and murdering day and night will let him have no peace, within or without, as the Scriptures picture him in **John 8** and **16; 1 Peter 5; Ephesians 6;** and **2 Timothy 2.**

Note: These questions and answers are no child's play, but are drawn up with great earnestness of purpose by the venerable and devout Dr. Luther for both young and old. Let each one pay attention and consider it a serious matter; for St. Paul writes to the Galatians in chapter six: "Do not be deceived: God cannot be mocked."

AN EXPLANATION
OF THE
SMALL CATECHISM

Designed to help students understand and apply Luther's Small Catechism, the following explanation section, like those found in earlier editions, was not written by Dr. Luther. An explanation section, however, has regularly accompanied editions of Luther's Small Catechism since the early days of Lutheranism. This explanation has been based upon and largely includes the work of Johann Konrad Dietrich (1575–1639), Carl Ferdinand Wilhelm Walther (1811–1887), Heinrich Christian Schwan (1819–1905), and the committee that prepared the synodical catechism of 1943.

INTRODUCTION

1. What is Christianity?

Christianity is the life and salvation God has given in and through Jesus Christ.

1   **John 14:6** I am the way and the truth and the life. No one comes to the Father except through Me.

2   **John 17:3** This is eternal life: that they may know You, the only true God, and Jesus Christ, whom You have sent.

3   **Acts 4:12** Salvation is found in no one else, for there is no other name under heaven given to men by which we must be saved.

4   **Acts 11:26** The disciples were called Christians first at Antioch.

5   **1 John 5:11–12** God has given us eternal life, and this life is in His Son. He who has the Son has life;

he who does not have the Son of God does not have life.

Note: Christianity was at first called "the Way" **(Acts 9:2; 24:14, 22).**

2. Where is God's truth about our Savior Jesus Christ made known?

This truth is made known in the Bible: the Old Testament, which promises the coming Savior, and the New Testament, which tells of the Savior who has come.

6   **Heb. 1:1–2** In the past God spoke to our forefathers through the prophets at many times and in various ways, but in these last days He has spoken to us by His Son.

7   **Luke 24:27** Beginning with Moses and all the Prophets, He explained to them what was said in all the Scriptures concerning Himself.

8   **John 20:31** These are written that you may believe that Jesus is the Christ, the Son of God, and that by believing you may have life in His name.

9   **Eph. 2:20** [You are] built on the foundation of the apostles and prophets, with Christ Jesus Himself as the chief cornerstone.

10   **1 John 1:1** That which was from the beginning, which we have heard, which we have seen with our eyes, which we have looked at and our hands have touched—this we proclaim concerning the Word of life.

3. Why do we call the Bible the "Holy Scripture"?

The Bible is the "Holy Scripture" because God the Holy Spirit gave to His chosen writers the thoughts that they expressed and the words that they wrote (verbal inspiration). Therefore, the Bible is God's own Word and truth, without error (inerrancy).

11   **John 10:35** The Scripture cannot be broken.

12   **Mark 8:38** If anyone is ashamed of Me and of My words in this adulterous and sinful generation, the Son of Man will be ashamed of him when He comes in His Father's glory with the holy angels.

13   **John 14:26** The Counselor, the Holy Spirit, whom the Father will send in My name, will teach you all things and will remind you of everything I have said to you.

14   **Acts 24:14** I admit that I worship the God of our fathers as a follower of the Way, which they call a sect. I believe everything that agrees with the Law and that is written in the Prophets.

15   **2 Tim. 3:16–17** All Scripture is God-breathed and is useful for teaching, rebuking, correcting and training in righteousness, so that the man of God may be thoroughly equipped for every good work.

16   **2 Peter 1:21** Prophecy never had its origin in the will of man, but men spoke from God as they were carried along by the Holy Spirit.

Note: God gave the Old Testament in Hebrew and Aramaic and the New Testament in Greek. Errors in copying or translations are not part of the God-breathed (inspired) Scripture.

4. What is the key to the correct understanding of the Bible?

Jesus Christ, the Savior of the world, is the heart and center of the Scripture and therefore the key to its true meaning.

17   **John 5:39** These are the Scriptures that testify about Me.

18   **Acts 10:43** All the prophets testify about Him that everyone who believes in Him receives forgiveness of sins through His name.

19   **John 1:18** No one has ever seen God, but God the One and Only, who is at the Father's side, has made Him known.

20   **2 Tim. 3:15** From infancy you have known the holy Scriptures, which are able to make you wise for salvation through faith in Christ Jesus.

Bible narrative: Jesus revealed Himself as the center of Scripture **(Luke 24:13–27).**

5. How is human reason to be used in understanding Holy Scripture?

A. Holy Scripture is given in human language. To determine what it says we need to apply the rules of language, such as grammar and logic. It is right to use reason as a servant of the text, but the guidance of the Holy Spirit is essential for its proper understanding.

21   **Ps. 119:73** Give me understanding to learn Your commands.

22   **Matt. 13:19** When anyone hears the message about the kingdom and does not understand it, the evil one comes and snatches away what was sown in his heart.

23   **Matt. 22:37** Love the Lord your God with all your heart and with all your soul and with all your mind.

24   **Acts 17:11** They received the message with great eagerness and examined the Scriptures every day to see if what Paul said was true.

B. Unlike all other books, Holy Scripture is God's

Word and truth. It is wrong to question or deny the truthfulness of the sacred text (as happens, for example, with historical criticism).

25 **Rom. 3:4** Let God be true, and every man a liar. As it is written: "So that you may be proved right when you speak and prevail when you judge."

26 **2 Cor. 10:5** We demolish arguments and every pretension that sets itself up against the knowledge of God.

27 **Col. 2:8** See to it that no one takes you captive through hollow and deceptive philosophy.

28 **2 Peter 3:15–16** Our dear brother Paul also wrote you with the wisdom that God gave him. He writes the same way in all his letters, speaking in them of these matters. His letters contain some things that are hard to understand, which ignorant and unstable people distort, as they do the other Scriptures, to their own destruction.

Note: See **1 Corinthians 1** and **2.**

6. What basic distinction must we keep in mind in order to understand the Bible?

We must sharply distinguish between the Law and the Gospel in the Bible.

29 **John 1:17** The law was given through Moses; grace and truth came through Jesus Christ.

30 **2 Cor. 3:6** The letter kills, but the Spirit gives life.

7. What does God teach and do in the Law?

In the Law God commands good works of thought, word, and deed and condemns and punishes sin.

31 **Mark 12:30–31** Love the Lord your God with all your heart and with all your soul and with all your

mind and with all your strength. . . . Love your neighbor as yourself.

32   **John 5:45** Your accuser is Moses, on whom your hopes are set.

33   **Rom. 3:20** Through the law we become conscious of sin.

8. What does God teach and do in the Gospel?

In the Gospel, the good news of our salvation in Jesus Christ, God gives forgiveness, faith, life, and the power to please Him with good works.

34   **John 3:16** God so loved the world that He gave His one and only Son, that whoever believes in Him shall not perish but have eternal life.

35   **John 6:63** The words I have spoken to you are spirit and they are life.

36   **Rom. 1:16** I am not ashamed of the gospel, because it is the power of God for the salvation of everyone who believes.

37   **Col. 1:6** All over the world this gospel is bearing fruit and growing, just as it has been doing among you since the day you heard it and understood God's grace in all its truth.

9. How does the Small Catechism sum up Christian doctrine?

The Small Catechism sums up Christian doctrine by dividing it into six chief parts: the Ten Commandments, the Creed, the Lord's Prayer, the Sacrament of Holy Baptism, Confession, and the Sacrament of the Altar.

10. What is a catechism?

A catechism is a book of instruction, usually in the form of questions and answers.

Note: A related word is *catechumen* (learner).

11. Who wrote our Small Catechism?

Martin Luther, the Reformer of the church, wrote the Small Catechism in 1529.

12. Why are all six chief parts of the Small Catechism taken from the Bible alone?

All the chief parts of the Small Catechism are taken from the Bible, because as God's written Word the Bible is the only final authority for Christian faith and life.

"We pledge ourselves to the prophetic and apostolic writings of the Old and New Testaments as the pure and clear fountain of Israel, which is the only true norm according to which all teachers and teachings are to be judged and evaluated. . . .

"[We have] a single, universally accepted . . . form of doctrine . . . from which and according to which, because it is drawn from the Word of God, all other writings are to be approved and accepted, judged and regulated" (Formula of Concord SD Rule and Norm 3, 10).

38   **Matt. 15:9** They worship Me in vain; their teachings are but rules taught by men.

39   **Gal. 1:8** Even if we or an angel from heaven should preach a gospel other than the one we preached to you, let him be eternally condemned.

—— THE TEN COMMANDMENTS ——

13. What are the Ten Commandments?

The Ten Commandments are the Law of God.

Note: God gave them in this order but did not number them **(Deut. 5:6–21; Ex. 20:1–17).**

14. How did God give His Law?

When God created people, He wrote the Law on their hearts. Later he arranged the Law in Ten Commandments, wrote it on two tables of stone, and made it known through Moses.

40 **Rom. 2:14–15** Indeed, when Gentiles, who do not have the law, do by nature things required by the law, they are a law for themselves, even though they do not have the law, since they show that the requirements of the law are written on their hearts,

their consciences also bearing witness, and their thoughts now accusing, now even defending them.

Bible narrative: God wrote His commandments directly for the Israelites **(Ex. 19–20; 31:18).** There are three kinds of laws in the Old Testament: the moral law, which tells all people their duty toward God and other people; the ceremonial law, which regulated the religious practices in the Old Testament; and the political law, which was the state law of the Israelites. Only the moral law was written into the human heart.

15. What is the summary of commandments 1–3 (First Table)?

Jesus replied: "Love the Lord your God with all your heart and with all your soul and with all your mind" **(Matt. 22:37;** see **Deut. 6:5).**

16. What is the summary of commandments 4–10 (Second Table)?

"And the second is like it: Love your neighbor as yourself" **(Matt. 22:39;** see **Lev. 19:18).**

17. What is the summary of all the commandments?

Love is the summary of all the commandments.

41   **Rom. 13:10** Love does no harm to its neighbor. Therefore love is the fulfillment of the law.

18. Whom does God mean when in the Ten Commandments He says, "You shall"?

He means me and all other human beings.

42   **Matt. 5:19** Anyone who breaks one of the least of these commandments and teaches others to do the same will be called least in the kingdom of heaven,

but whoever practices and teaches these commands will be called great in the kingdom of heaven.

43   **Rom. 3:19** Now we know that whatever the law says, it says to those who are under the law, so that every mouth may be silenced and the whole world held accountable to God.

Bible narrative: Jesus explained the meaning of these commandments for all people **(Matthew 5).**

The First Commandment

[God]

You shall have no other gods.

What does this mean? We should fear, love, and trust in God above all things.

19. Who is the only true God?

The only true God is the triune God: Father, Son, and Holy Spirit, three distinct persons in one divine being (the Holy Trinity).

44   **Num. 6:24–26** The Lord bless you and keep you; the Lord make His face shine upon you and be gracious to you; the Lord turn His face toward you and give you peace.

45   **Deut. 6:4** Hear, O Israel: The Lord our God, the Lord is one.

46   **Matt. 28:19** Go and make disciples of all nations, baptizing them in the name of the Father and of the Son and of the Holy Spirit.

47   **1 Cor. 8:4** There is no God but one.

48   **2 Cor. 13:14** May the grace of the Lord Jesus Christ, and the love of God, and the fellowship of the Holy Spirit be with you all.

Bible narrative: At His Baptism Jesus stood in the Jordan, the Father spoke from heaven, and the Spirit of God descended upon Jesus in the form of a dove **(Matt. 3:16–17)**.

20. What does God forbid in the First Commandment?

God forbids us to have other gods (idolatry).

49   **Is. 42:8** I am the Lord; that is My name! I will not give My glory to another or My praise to idols.

50   **Matt. 4:10** Worship the Lord your God, and serve Him only.

51   **1 Cor. 8:4** We know that an idol is nothing at all in the world and that there is no God but one.

52   **1 John 5:21** Dear children, keep yourselves from idols.

21. When do people have other gods?

They have other gods

A. when they regard and worship any creature or thing as God;

53   **Ps. 115:4** Their idols are silver and gold.

54   **Phil. 3:19** Their destiny is destruction, their god is their stomach, and their glory is in their shame. Their mind is on earthly things.

55   **Rev. 9:20** They did not stop worshiping demons, and idols of gold, silver, bronze, stone and wood— idols that cannot see or hear or walk.

Bible narratives: Israel worshiped the golden calf **(Exodus 32)**. The people worshiped Baal **(1 Kings 18:18–29)**. The Philistines made Dagon their god **(Judges 16:23–24)**.

B. when they believe in a god who is not the triune God (see the Apostles' Creed);

56   **Matt. 28:19** Go and make disciples of all nations, baptizing them in the name of the Father and of the Son and of the Holy Spirit.

57   **John 5:23** He who does not honor the Son does not honor the Father, who sent Him.

Bible narrative: The Baptism of Jesus **(Matt. 3:13–17).**

C. when they fear, love, or trust in any person or thing as they should fear, love, and trust in God alone;

58   **Ps. 14:1** The fool says in his heart, "There is no God." They are corrupt, their deeds are vile; there is no one who does good.

59   **Prov. 11:28** Whoever trusts in his riches will fall.

60   **Prov. 3:5** Trust in the Lord with all your heart and lean not on your own understanding.

61   **Matt. 10:28** Do not be afraid of those who kill the body but cannot kill the soul. Rather, be afraid of the One who can destroy both soul and body in hell.

62   **Matt. 10:37** Anyone who loves his father or mother more than Me is not worthy of Me; anyone who loves his son or daughter more than Me is not worthy of Me.

63   **Eph. 5:5** No immoral, impure or greedy person—such a man is an idolater—has any inheritance in the kingdom of Christ and of God.

Bible narratives: The rich man thought more of costly clothes and good eating than of God **(Luke 16:19–31).** The people building the Tower of Babel considered their achievement more important than God **(Gen. 11:1–9).** Goliath trusted in his size and physical strength **(1 Sam. 17).** Eli honored his sons more than God **(1 Sam. 2:**

12–34). Peter feared punishment more than he loved God **(Matt. 26:69–75).**

D. when they join in the worship of one who is not the triune God.

64   **2 Cor. 6:14–15** Do not be yoked together with unbelievers. For what do righteousness and wickedness have in common? Or what fellowship can light have with darkness? What harmony is there between Christ and Belial? What does a believer have in common with an unbeliever?

22. What does God require of us in the First Commandment?

God requires that we fear, love, and trust in Him above all things.

A. We fear God above all things when we revere Him alone as the highest being, honor Him with our lives, and avoid what displeases Him.

65   **Gen. 17:1** I am God almighty; walk before Me and be blameless.

66   **Ps. 33:8** Let all the earth fear the Lord; let all the people of the world revere Him.

67   **Ps. 96:4** Great is the Lord and most worthy of praise; He is to be feared above all gods.

68   **Prov. 8:13** To fear the Lord is to hate evil.

69   **Matt. 10:28** Do not be afraid of those who kill the body but cannot kill the soul. Rather, be afraid of the One who can destroy both soul and body in hell.

Bible narrative: The three men in the fiery furnace feared God more than the king **(Daniel 3).**

B. We love God above all things when we cling to Him alone as our God and gladly devote our lives to His service.

70   **Ps. 73:25–26** Whom have I in heaven but You? And earth has nothing I desire besides You. My flesh and my heart may fail, but God is the strength of my heart and my portion forever.

71   **Matt. 22:37** Love the Lord your God with all your heart and with all your soul and with all your mind.

Bible narrative: Abraham loved God more than his son **(Genesis 22).** Joseph resisted the temptation of Potiphar's wife **(Genesis 39).**

C. We trust in God above all things when we commit our lives completely to His keeping and rely on Him for help in every need.

72   **Ps. 118:8** It is better to take refuge in the Lord than to trust in man.

73   **Prov. 3:5** Trust in the Lord with all your heart and lean not on your own understanding.

Bible narrative: David trusted in the Lord when he fought against Goliath **(1 Sam. 17:37, 46–47).** Abram left his country and relatives to go where the Lord sent him, trusting that the Lord would take care of him **(Gen. 12:1–9).** Daniel committed himself to the Lord's keeping **(Daniel 6).**

23. Who is able to keep this and the other commandments?

No person can keep any or all commandments perfectly, except Jesus Christ. All those who have faith in Him by the power of His Spirit willingly strive to keep these commandments.

74   **Eccl. 7:20** There is not a righteous man on earth who does what is right and never sins.

75   **1 John 1:8** If we claim to be without sin, we deceive ourselves and the truth is not in us.

76   **John 14:15** If you love me, you will obey what I command.

77   **Phil. 2:13** It is God who works in you to will and to act according to His good purpose.

The Second Commandment

[God's Name]

You shall not misuse the name of the Lord your God.

What does this mean? We should fear and love God so that we do not curse, swear, use satanic arts, lie, or deceive by His name, but call upon it in every trouble, pray, praise, and give thanks.

24. Why do we say in this and in the following commandments, "We should fear and love God"?

The fulfillment of all commandments must flow from the fear and love of God.

78   **Ps. 111:10** The fear of the Lord is the beginning of wisdom; all who follow His precepts have good understanding. To Him belongs eternal praise.

79   **John 14:23** If anyone loves Me, he will obey My teaching.

Bible narrative: Jesus asked Peter whether he loved Him, then He told Peter to feed His sheep **(John 21: 15–17)**.

25. What is God's name?

God, as He has revealed Himself to us, His essence and His attributes.

80   **Ex. 3:14** God said to Moses, "I AM WHO I AM." This is what you are to say to the Israelites: "I AM has sent me to you."

81   **Is. 9:6** To us a child is born, to us a son is given, and the government will be on His shoulders. And He will be called Wonderful Counselor, Mighty God, Everlasting Father, Prince of Peace.

82   **Jer. 23:6** This is the name by which He will be called: The Lord Our Righteousness.

83   **Matt. 1:21** You are to give Him the name Jesus, because He will save His people from their sins.

84   **Matt. 18:20** Where two or three come together in My name, there am I with them.

85   **Matt. 28:19** Go and make disciples of all nations, baptizing them in the name of the Father and of the Son and of the Holy Spirit.

86   **John 1:1** In the beginning was the Word, and the Word was with God, and the Word was God.

Bible narrative: God revealed His name to Moses **(Ex. 3:12–15).**

26. What does God forbid in the Second Commandment?

In the Second Commandment God forbids us to misuse His name.

87   **Ex. 20:7** The Lord will not hold anyone guiltless who misuses His name.

27. How is God's name misused?

God's name is misused when people

A. speak God's name uselessly or carelessly (see **Ex. 20:7**);

B. curse, swear, use satanic arts, lie, or deceive by His name.

28. What is cursing by God's name?

Cursing by God's name is

A. blaspheming God by speaking evil of Him or mocking Him;

88   **Lev. 24:15** If anyone curses his God, he will be held responsible.

Bible narratives: They mocked Jesus when He was hanging on the cross **(Matt. 27:39–43).** The Assyrian field commander blasphemed the God of Israel **(2 Kings 18:28–35; 19:21–22).** Some Jews accused Jesus of being possessed by a demon **(John 8:48–59).**

B. calling down the anger and punishment of God upon oneself or any other person or thing.

89   **James 3:9–10** With the tongue we praise our Lord and Father, and with it we curse men, who have been made in God's likeness. Out of the same mouth come praise and cursing. My brothers, this should not be.

Bible narratives: The people at Jesus' trial cursed themselves and their children **(Matt. 27:25).** Peter cursed **(Matt. 26:74).** James and John asked Jesus if they should ask God to destroy a Samaritan village **(Luke 9:51–55).**

29. What is swearing by God's name?

Swearing by God's name is taking an oath in which we call on God to witness the truth of what we say or promise and to punish us if we lie or break our promise.

30. When are we permitted, and even required, to swear by God's name?

We are permitted, and even required, to take an oath

by God's name when an oath is necessary for the glory of God or the welfare of our neighbor. Examples include the following: testimony in court, oath of office, wedding vows.

90   **Rom. 13:1** Everyone must submit himself to the governing authorities.

91   **Num. 30:2** When a man makes a vow to the Lord or takes an oath to obligate himself by a pledge, he must not break his word but must do everything he said.

92   **Deut. 6:13** Fear the Lord your God, serve Him only and take your oaths in His name.

93   **Heb. 6:16** Men swear by someone greater than themselves, and the oath confirms what is said and puts an end to all argument.

Bible narratives: Jesus permitted Himself to be put under oath **(Matt. 26:63–64)**. Abraham put his servant under oath **(Gen. 24:3)**.

31. When is swearing forbidden?

Swearing is forbidden when it is done falsely, thoughtlessly, or in sinful, uncertain, or unimportant matters.

94   **Lev. 19:12** Do not swear falsely by My name and so profane the name of your God. I am the Lord.

95   **Matt. 5:33–37** You have heard that it was said to the people long ago, "Do not break your oath but keep the oaths you have made to the Lord." But I tell you, Do not swear at all: either by heaven, for it is God's throne, or by the earth, for it is His footstool; or by Jerusalem, for it is the city of the Great King. And do not swear by your head, for you cannot make even one hair white or black. Simply let your

"Yes" be "Yes" and your "No," "No"; anything beyond this comes from the evil one.

Bible narratives: Peter swore falsely and thus committed perjury **(Matt. 26:72)**. Certain Jews swore to commit murder **(Acts 23:12)**. Herod swore in an unknown and unimportant matter **(Matt. 14:6–9)**. Jephthah's thoughtless oath **(Judges 11:30–40)**.

32. What is using satanic arts by God's name?

Using satanic arts by God's name is

A. using God's name in order to perform or claim to perform supernatural things with the help of the devil, such as casting spells, calling up a spirit, fortune-telling, consulting the dead, or other occult practices;

96   **Deut. 18:10–12** Let no one be found among you who sacrifices his son or daughter in the fire, who practices divination or sorcery, interprets omens, engages in witchcraft, or casts spells, or who is a medium or spiritist or who consults the dead. Anyone who does these things is detestable to the Lord, and because of these detestable practices the Lord your God will drive out those nations before you.

Bible narratives: The Egyptian sorcerers performed supernatural things with the help of the devil **(Exodus 7–8)**. The sons of Sceva used Jesus' name to cast out spirits, but they did not have faith **(Acts 19:13–29)**.

B. joining with or seeking the aid of people who practice these and similar satanic arts or worship Satan;

97   **Lev. 19:31** Do not turn to mediums or seek out spiritists, for you will be defiled by them. I am the Lord your God.

Bible narrative: King Saul sought the help of the witch of Endor **(1 Samuel 28).**

C. depending on horoscopes or similar ways to foretell the future.

98   **Eccl. 7:14** When times are good, be happy; but when times are bad, consider: God has made the one as well as the other. Therefore, a man cannot discover anything about his future.

33. What is lying and deceiving by God's name?

Lying and deceiving by God's name is

A. teaching false doctrine and saying that it is God's Word or revelation;

99   **Deut. 12:32** See that you do all I command you; do not add to it or take away from it.
100   **Jer. 23:31** Yes, declares the Lord, I am against the prophets who wag their own tongues and yet declare, "The Lord declares."
101   **Matt. 15:9** They worship me in vain; their teachings are but rules taught by men.

Bible narrative: The lie of a false prophet caused a prophet of God to be deceived and killed **(1 Kings 13: 11–30).**

B. covering up an unbelieving heart or a sinful life by pretending to be a Christian.

102   **Matt. 7:21** Not everyone who says to Me, "Lord, Lord," will enter the kingdom of heaven, but only he who does the will of My Father who is in heaven.
103   **Matt. 15:8** These people honor Me with their lips, but their hearts are far from Me.

Bible narratives: Many scribes and Pharisees were hypocrites **(Matt. 23:13–33).** Ananias and Sapphira were hypocrites **(Acts 5:1–11).**

34. What does God require of us in the Second Commandment?

We should call upon His name in every trouble, pray, praise, and give thanks.

104   **Ps. 50:15** Call upon Me in the day of trouble; I will deliver you, and you will honor Me.

105   **Ps. 103:1** Praise the Lord, O my soul; all my inmost being, praise His holy name.

106   **Ps. 118:1** Give thanks to the Lord, for He is good; His love endures forever.

107   **John 16:23** My Father will give you whatever you ask in My name.

108   **Eph. 5:20** Give thanks to God the Father for everything, in the name of our Lord Jesus Christ.

Bible narratives: The 10 lepers called upon Jesus in their trouble **(Luke 17:11–13).** The grateful stranger thanked Jesus and glorified God for the healing **(Luke 17:15–16).** Hannah petitioned and thanked God for the gift of a son **(1 Samuel 1–2).** Mary's Song (Magnificat, **Luke 1:46–55**). Zechariah's Song (Benedictus, **Luke 1:68–79**).

The Third Commandment

[God's Word]

Remember the Sabbath day by keeping it holy.

What does this mean? We should fear and love God so that we do not despise preaching and His Word, but hold it sacred and gladly hear and learn it.

35. What is the Sabbath day?

In the Old Testament God set aside the seventh day

(Saturday) as a required day of rest (*Sabbath* means "rest") and worship.

109   **Ex. 35:2** For six days, work is to be done, but the seventh day shall be your holy day, a Sabbath of rest to the Lord.

110   **Lev. 23:3** There are six days when you may work, but the seventh day is a holy day, a Sabbath of rest, a day of sacred assembly.

36. Does God require us to observe the Sabbath and other holy days of the Old Testament?

The Sabbath was a sign pointing to Jesus, who is our rest. Since Jesus has come as our Savior and Lord, God no longer requires us to observe the Sabbath day and other holy days of the Old Testament.

111   **Matt. 11:28** "Come to me, all you who are weary and burdened, and I will give you rest."

112   **Matt. 12:8** "The Son of Man is Lord of the Sabbath."

113   **Col. 2:16–17** Do not let anyone judge you by what you eat or drink, or with regard to a religious festival, a New Moon celebration or a Sabbath day. These are a shadow of the things that were to come; the reality, however, is found in Christ.

114   **Heb. 4:9–10** There remains, then, a Sabbath-rest for the people of God; for anyone who enters God's rest also rests from his own work, just as God did from His.

37. Does God require the church to worship together on any specific days?

A. God requires Christians to worship together.

115   **Acts 2:42, 46** They devoted themselves to the apostles' teaching and to the fellowship, to the breaking

of bread and to prayer. . . . Every day they continued to meet together in the temple courts. They broke bread in their homes and ate together with glad and sincere hearts.

116 **Heb. 10:25** Let us not give up meeting together, as some are in the habit of doing, but let us encourage one another—and all the more as you see the Day approaching.

B. He has not specified any particular day.

117 **Rom. 14:5–6** One man considers one day more sacred than another; another man considers every day alike. Each one should be fully convinced in his own mind. He who regards one day as special, does so to the Lord.

118 **Gal. 4:10–11** You are observing special days and months and seasons and years! I fear for you, that somehow I have wasted my efforts on you.

C. The church worships together especially on Sunday because Christ rose from the dead on Sunday.

119 **Luke 24:1–2** On the first day of the week, very early in the morning, the women took the spices they had prepared and went to the tomb. They found the stone rolled away from the tomb.

120 **Acts 20:7** On the first day of the week we came together to break bread. Paul spoke to the people and, because he intended to leave the next day, kept on talking until midnight.

Bible narrative: Jesus appeared to His disciples **(John 20:19–31).**

38. When do we sin against the Third Commandment?

We sin against the Third Commandment when we despise preaching and the Word of God.

39. How is this done?

We despise preaching and the Word of God

A. when we do not attend public worship;

B. when we do not use the Word of God and the Sacraments;

C. when we use the Word of God and the Sacraments negligently or carelessly.

121   **John 8:47** He who belongs to God hears what God says. The reason you do not hear is that you do not belong to God.

122   **Luke 10:16** He who listens to you listens to Me; he who rejects you rejects Me; but he who rejects Me rejects Him who sent Me.

Bible narratives: The scribes and the Pharisees despised Baptism **(Luke 7:30).** Saul rejected the Word of God **(1 Sam. 15:10–23).**

40. What does God require of us in the Third Commandment?

A. We should hold preaching and the Word of God sacred.

123   **Is. 66:2** This is the one I esteem: he who is humble and contrite in spirit, and trembles at My word.

124   **1 Thess. 2:13** When you received the word of God, which you heard from us, you accepted it not as the word of men, but as it actually is, the word of God, which is at work in you who believe.

B. We should gladly hear it, learn it, and meditate on it.

125   **Joshua 1:8** Do not let this Book of the Law depart from your mouth; meditate on it day and night, so that you may be careful to do everything written in it.

126   **Ps. 26:8** I love the house where You live, O Lord, the place where Your glory dwells.

127   **Luke 11:28** Blessed rather are those who hear the word of God and obey it.

128   **Acts 2:42** They devoted themselves to the apostles' teaching and to the fellowship, to the breaking of bread and to prayer.

129   **Col. 3:16** Let the word of Christ dwell in you richly as you teach and admonish one another with all wisdom, and as you sing psalms, hymns and spiritual songs with gratitude in your hearts to God.

Bible narratives: Jesus gladly heard and learned the Word of God **(Luke 2:41–52).** Mary sat at the feet of Jesus and learned His Word **(Luke 10:39).** Mary kept and pondered the Word of God in her heart **(Luke 2:19).** The Bereans searched the Scriptures daily **(Acts 17:11).**

C. We should honor and support the preaching and teaching of the Word of God.

130   **Gal. 6:6–7** Anyone who receives instruction in the word must share all good things with his instructor. Do not be deceived: God cannot be mocked. A man reaps what he sows.

Bible narrative: The poor widow gave money for the upkeep of the temple and for the support of the priests **(Mark 12:41–44).**

Note: See also "What the Hearers Owe Their Pastors" under the Table of Duties.

D. We should diligently spread the Word of God.

131   **Mark 16:15** He said to them, "Go into all the world and preach the good news to all creation."

41. What do the first three commandments (the First Table) show us about ourselves?

That we have sinned and deserve God's condemnation.

132   **Rom. 3:22–23** There is no difference, for all have sinned and fall short of the glory of God.

42. Who alone has kept the Law of God perfectly?

Only Jesus Christ, the God-man.

133   **John 8:46** "Can any of you prove Me guilty of sin?"
134   **Heb. 4:15** We do not have a high priest who is unable to sympathize with our weaknesses, but we have one who has been tempted in every way, just as we are—yet without sin.

43. How does Christ's perfect keeping of the Law benefit us?

Since Christ was our substitute before God, our Savior's perfect keeping of the Law is part of His saving work for us, and because of Him we are considered righteous before God.

135   **Gal. 4:4–5** When the time had fully come, God sent His Son, born of a woman, born under law, to redeem those under law, that we might receive the full rights of sons.

44. Besides showing us our sin, what else does God's Law do for us?

In the Ten Commandments God shows us what His will is. Christians, by the power of the Holy Spirit, are eager to do God's will.

136   **1 Thess. 4:3** It is God's will that you should be sanctified.

45. What is the summary of commandments 4–10 (Second Table)?

"Love your neighbor as yourself " **(Matt. 22:39).**

46. Who is our neighbor?

All people are our neighbors.

137   **Gal. 6:10** As we have opportunity, let us do good to all people, especially to those who belong to the family of believers.
138   **Matt. 5:44** Love your enemies and pray for those who persecute you.

Bible narrative: The good Samaritan showed mercy to his neighbor **(Luke 10:25–37).**

47. How should we love our neighbor?

We should love our neighbor as ourselves and show this love by keeping the commandments of the Second Table.

139   **Matt. 7:12** In everything, do to others what you would have them do to you, for this sums up the Law and the Prophets.

The Fourth Commandment

[God's Representatives]

Honor your father and your mother.

What does this mean? We should fear and love God so that we do not despise or anger our parents and other authorities, but honor them, serve and obey them, love and cherish them.

48. Who are parents and other authorities?

Parents are fathers, mothers, and guardians; other authorities are all those whom God has placed over us at home, in government, at school, at the place where we work, and in the church.

Note: Regarding spiritual authority, see the Table of Duties, "What the Hearers Owe Their Pastors" and also "The Office of the Keys" under Confession.

49. What does God forbid in the Fourth Commandment?

God forbids us to despise our parents and other authorities by not respecting them or angering them by our disobedience or by any other kind of sin.

140   **Prov. 23:22** Listen to your father, who gave you life, and do not despise your mother when she is old.

141   **Rom. 13:2** He who rebels against the authority is rebelling against what God has instituted, and those who do so will bring judgment on themselves.

Note: See "To Workers of All Kinds" under the Table of Duties.

Bible narratives: The sons of Eli grieved their father by

their wickedness **(1 Sam. 2:12, 23, 25)**. Absalom rebelled against his father and king **(2 Samuel 15)**.

50. What does God require of us in the Fourth Commandment?

God requires us

A. to honor our parents and other authorities by regarding them as God's representatives;

142   **Eph. 6:2–3** "Honor your father and mother"— which is the first commandment with a promise— "that it may go well with you and that you may enjoy long life on the earth."

Note: See "To Parents" and "To Children" under the Table of Duties.

Bible narratives: Joseph honored his father **(Gen. 46:29)**. King Solomon honored his mother **(1 Kings 2:19)**. Elisha honored his teacher **(2 Kings 2:12)**.

B. to serve our parents and other authorities by gladly providing what they need or require;

143   **1 Tim. 5:4** If a widow has children or grandchildren, these should learn first of all to put their religion into practice by caring for their own family and so repaying their parents and grandparents, for this is pleasing to God.

144   **Rom. 13:7** Give everyone what you owe him: If you owe taxes, pay taxes; if revenue, then revenue; if respect, then respect; if honor, then honor.

Bible narratives: Joseph provided for his father **(Gen. 47:11–12)**. Jesus provided for His mother **(John 19:26)**.

C. to obey our parents and other authorities in everything in which God has placed them over us;

145   **Col. 3:20** Children, obey your parents in every-
       thing, for this pleases the Lord.
146   **Titus 3:1** Remind the people to be subject to rulers
       and authorities, to be obedient, to be ready to do
       whatever is good.
147   **Acts 5:29** We must obey God rather than men!

Note: See "To Workers of All Kinds," "To Employers
and Supervisors," and "Of Citizens" in the Table of
Duties.

Bible narratives: Jesus was subject to Mary and Joseph
(Luke 2:51). Jonathan disobeyed his father in order to
spare David's life and thus obeyed God rather than man
(1 Sam. 20:31–33).

D. to love and cherish our parents and other authorities as precious gifts of God;

148   **Prov. 23:22** Listen to your father, who gave you life,
       and do not despise your mother when she is old.

Bible narrative: Ruth loved and cherished her mother-
in-law, Naomi **(Ruth).**

E. to show respect to the aged.

149   **Lev. 19:32** Rise in the presence of the aged, show
       respect for the elderly and revere your God.

*51. What promise does God attach to this command-
ment?*

. . . that it may go well with you and that you may
enjoy long life on the earth. **Eph. 6:3**

The Fifth Commandment

[God's Gift of Life]

You shall not murder.

What does this mean? We should fear and love God so that we do not hurt or harm our neighbor in his body, but help and support him in every physical need.

52. What does God forbid in the Fifth Commandment?

A. God forbids us to take the life of another person (murder, abortion, euthanasia) or our own life (suicide).

150   **Gen. 9:6** Whoever sheds the blood of man, by man shall his blood be shed; for in the image of God has God made man.

151   **Matt. 26:52** All who draw the sword will die by the sword.

Bible narratives: Cain murdered his brother Abel **(Gen. 4:8).** David murdered Uriah through others **(2 Sam. 11:15).** Killing through carelessness **(Ex. 21:29** and **Deut. 22:8).** Judas killed himself **(Matt. 27:5).**

ABORTION

The living but unborn are persons in the sight of God from the time of conception. Since abortion takes a human life, it is not a moral option except to prevent the death of another person, the mother.

152   **Jer. 1:5** Before I formed you in the womb I knew you, before you were born I set you apart.

153   **Ps. 139:16** Your eyes saw my unformed body. All the days ordained for me were written in Your book before one of them came to be.

Bible narrative: John the Baptist leaped for joy while still in his mother's womb. In doing so, John the Baptist and Elizabeth, by the Holy Spirit, acknowledged the unborn Jesus as Lord **(Luke 1:41–44).**

EUTHANASIA

The severely handicapped, infirm, helpless, and aged are persons in the sight of God with life given by Him and to be ended only by Him.

154   **Prov. 6:16–17** There are six things the Lord hates, seven that are detestable to Him: haughty eyes, a lying tongue, hands that shed innocent blood.

155   **Prov. 31:8** Speak up for those who cannot speak for themselves, for the rights of all who are destitute.

156   **Acts 17:25** He Himself gives all men life and breath and everything else.

SUICIDE

My own life is a gift of God to be ended only by Him.

157   **Jer. 31:3** The Lord appeared to us in the past, saying: "I have loved you with an everlasting love; I have drawn you with loving-kindness."

158   **Luke 12:22** Jesus said to His disciples: "Therefore I tell you, do not worry about your life, what you will eat; or about your body, what you will wear."

B. God forbids us to hurt or harm our neighbor physically, that is, to do or say anything which may destroy, shorten, or make his or her life bitter.

159   **Deut. 32:39** See now that I Myself am He! There is no god besides Me. I put to death and I bring to life,

I have wounded and I will heal, and no one can deliver out of My hand.

160   **Rom. 12:19** Do not take revenge, my friends, but leave room for God's wrath, for it is written: "It is Mine to avenge; I will repay," says the Lord.

Bible narratives: Joseph's brothers harmed Joseph and made the life of their father bitter by their wickedness **(Gen. 37:23–35).** The Egyptians made the lives of the children of Israel bitter by hard labor **(Exodus 1).**

C. God forbids us to keep anger and hatred in our hearts against our neighbor.

161   **Matt. 5:22** I tell you that anyone who is angry with his brother will be subject to judgment.

162   **1 John 3:15** Anyone who hates his brother is a murderer, and you know that no murderer has eternal life in him.

163   **Matt. 15:19** Out of the heart come evil thoughts, murder, adultery, sexual immorality, theft, false testimony, slander.

164   **Eph. 4:26** In your anger do not sin: Do not let the sun go down while you are still angry.

Bible narratives: The Jews showed their anger against Stephen **(Acts 7:54).** God warned Cain against anger **(Gen. 4:5–7).**

53. Does anyone have authority to take another person's life?

Yes, lawful government, as God's servant, may execute criminals and fight just wars.

165   **Rom. 13:4** He is God's servant to do you good. But if you do wrong, be afraid, for he does not bear the sword for nothing. He is God's servant, an agent of wrath to bring punishment on the wrongdoer.

54. What does God require of us in the Fifth Commandment?

A. We should help and support our neighbor in every bodily need.

166   **Rom. 12:20** If your enemy is hungry, feed him; if he is thirsty, give him something to drink. In doing this, you will heap burning coals on his head.

Bible narratives: Abraham rescued Lot from his enemies **(Gen. 14:12–16).** David protected the life of Saul **(1 Sam. 26:1–12).** The good Samaritan helped the man who had fallen among thieves **(Luke 10:33–35).**

B. We should be merciful, kind, and forgiving towards our neighbor.

167   **Matt. 5:5, 7, 9** Blessed are the meek, for they will inherit the earth. . . . Blessed are the merciful, for they will be shown mercy. . . . Blessed are the peacemakers, for they will be called sons of God.

168   **Matt. 6:15** If you do not forgive men their sins, your Father will not forgive your sins.

169   **Eph. 4:32** Be kind and compassionate to one another, forgiving each other, just as in Christ God forgave you.

Bible narratives: Jesus showed mercy to the 10 lepers **(Luke 17:11–19).** The centurion was kind to his sick servant **(Matt. 8:5–13).** Joseph was forgiving toward his brothers **(Gen. 45:1–16).**

C. We should avoid and assist our neighbor in avoiding the abuse of drugs and the use of any substance that harms the body and the mind.

170   **2 Cor. 7:1** Let us purify ourselves from everything that contaminates body and spirit.

The Sixth Commandment

[God's Gift of Marriage]

You shall not commit adultery.

What does this mean? We should fear and love God so that we lead a sexually pure and decent life in what we say and do, and husband and wife love and honor each other.

55. How do we lead a sexually pure and decent life?

We lead a sexually pure and decent life when we
A. consider sexuality to be a good gift of God;

171 **Gen. 1:27, 31** God created man in His own image, in the image of God He created him; male and female He created them. . . . God saw all that He had made, and it was very good.

B. honor marriage as God's institution, the lifelong union of one man and one woman;

172 **Gen. 2:24–25** For this reason a man will leave his father and mother and be united to his wife, and they will become one flesh. The man and his wife were both naked, and they felt no shame.

173 **Mark 10:6–9** At the beginning of creation God "made them male and female." For this reason a man will leave his father and mother and be united to his wife, and the two will become one flesh. So they are no longer two, but one. Therefore what God has joined together, let man not separate.

C. reserve sexual intercourse for the marriage partner alone;

174   **Heb. 13:4** Marriage should be honored by all, and
        the marriage bed kept pure, for God will judge the
        adulterer and all the sexually immoral.

D. control sexual urges in a God-pleasing way.

175   **Titus 2:11–12** The grace of God that brings salva-
        tion has appeared to all men. It teaches us to say
        "No" to ungodliness and worldly passions, and to
        live self-controlled, upright and godly lives in this
        present age.

Note: See also **1 Thess. 4:1–7.**

*56. What does God forbid in the Sixth Command-
ment?*

A. God forbids divorce except for marital unfaithful-
ness (adultery or desertion).

176   **Matt. 19:6** They are no longer two, but one.
        Therefore what God has joined together, let man not
        separate.

177   **Matt. 19:9** Anyone who divorces his wife, except for
        marital unfaithfulness, and marries another woman
        commits adultery.

178   **1 Cor. 7:15** If the unbeliever leaves, let him do so.
        A believing man or woman is not bound in such
        circumstances.

Bible narratives: David committed adultery with the
wife of Uriah **(2 Samuel 11).** Herod took his brother's
wife **(Mark 6:18).**

B. God forbids sexual intercourse between unmarried
persons.

179   **1 Cor. 6:18** Flee from sexual immorality.

180   **1 Cor. 6:9–10** Neither the sexually immoral nor
        idolaters nor adulterers nor male prostitutes nor

homosexual offenders . . . will enter the kingdom of
God.

C. God forbids sexual sins such as rape, homosexual
activity, incest, sexual child abuse, obscenity, and the
use of pornographic materials.

181   **Rom. 1:24, 26–27** Therefore God gave them over
        in the sinful desires of their hearts to sexual impurity
        for the degrading of their bodies with one another.
        . . . Even their women exchanged natural relations
        for unnatural ones. In the same way the men also
        abandoned natural relations with women and were
        inflamed with lust for one another. Men committed
        indecent acts with other men, and received in them-
        selves the due penalty for their perversion.

182   **1 Cor. 6:9–10** Do you not know that the wicked
        will not inherit the kingdom of God? Do not be
        deceived: Neither the sexually immoral nor adul-
        terers nor male prostitutes nor homosexual
        offenders nor thieves nor the greedy nor drunkards
        nor slanderers nor swindlers will inherit the
        kingdom of God.

D. God forbids sexually impure thoughts and desires.

183   **Matt. 5:28** I tell you that anyone who looks at a
        woman lustfully has already committed adultery
        with her in his heart.

184   **Matt. 15:19** Out of the heart come evil thoughts,
        murder, adultery, sexual immorality, theft, false testi-
        mony, slander.

*57. What does God require of us in the Sixth Com-
mandment?*

A. God requires us to avoid all temptations to sexual
sin.

185   **Gen. 39:9** How then could I do such a wicked thing and sin against God?

186   **1 Cor. 6:18** Flee from sexual immorality. All other sins a man commits are outside his body, but he who sins sexually sins against his own body.

B. God requires us to be clean in what we think and say.

187   **Eph. 5:3–4** Among you there must not be even a hint of sexual immorality, or of any kind of impurity, or of greed, because these are improper for God's holy people. Nor should there be obscenity, foolish talk or coarse joking, which are out of place, but rather thanksgiving.

188   **Phil. 4:8** Finally, brothers, whatever is true, whatever is noble, whatever is right, whatever is pure, whatever is lovely, whatever is admirable—if anything is excellent or praiseworthy—think about such things.

C. God requires us to use our sexuality in ways pleasing to Him.

189   **1 Cor. 6:19–20** Do you not know that your body is a temple of the Holy Spirit, who is in you, whom you have received from God? You are not your own; you were bought at a price. Therefore honor God with your body.

58. What does God require especially of married people?

God requires married people to love, honor, and respect each other. The wife is the husband's God-given helper, and the husband is the wife's God-given head.

190   **Gen. 2:18** The Lord God said, "It is not good for the

man to be alone. I will make a helper suitable for him."

191   **1 Cor. 7:4** The wife's body does not belong to her alone but also to her husband. In the same way, the husband's body does not belong to him alone but also to his wife.

192   **Eph. 4:32** Be kind and compassionate to one another, forgiving each other, just as in Christ God forgave you.

193   **Eph. 5:21–23, 25** Submit to one another out of reverence for Christ. Wives, submit to your husbands as to the Lord. For the husband is the head of the wife as Christ is the head of the church, His body, of which He is the Savior. . . . Husbands, love your wives, just as Christ loved the church and gave Himself up for her.

Note: See "To Husbands" and "To Wives" under the Table of Duties.

The Seventh Commandment

[God's Gift of Possessions]

You shall not steal.

What does this mean? We should fear and love God so that we do not take our neighbor's money or possessions, or get them in any dishonest way, but help him to improve and protect his possessions and income.

59. What does God forbid in the Seventh Commandment?

God forbids every kind of robbery, theft, and dishonest way of getting things.

194   **Lev. 19:35** Do not use dishonest standards when measuring length, weight or quantity.

195   **Ps. 37:21** The wicked borrow and do not repay, but the righteous give generously.

196   **Eph. 4:28** He who has been stealing must steal no longer, but must work, doing something useful with his own hands, that he may have something to share with those in need.

197   **2 Thess. 3:10** If a man will not work, he shall not eat.

Bible narratives: Achan stole when he secretly took a garment and silver and gold **(Joshua 7:20–22)**. Judas was a thief **(John 12:6)**. Gehazi obtained a present by lying and trickery **(2 Kings 5:20–24)**.

60. What does God require of us in the Seventh Commandment?

A. We should help our neighbor to improve and protect that person's possessions and income.

198   **Matt. 7:12** In everything, do to others what you would have them do to you.

199   **Phil. 2:4** Each of you should look not only to your own interests, but also to the interests of others.

Bible narratives: Abraham gave Lot the choice of the land **(Gen. 13:9)**. Abraham rescued Lot from the enemy and recovered Lot's property **(Gen. 14:12–16)**.

B. We should help our neighbor in every need.

200   **Matt. 5:42** Give to the one who asks you, and do not turn away from the one who wants to borrow from you.

201   **Heb. 13:16** Do not forget to do good, and to share with others, for with such sacrifices God is pleased.

202   **1 John 3:17** If anyone has material possessions and sees his brother in need but has no pity on him, how can the love of God be in him?

Bible narratives: Zacchaeus promised to give back four times what he had taken dishonestly and to give half of his goods to the poor **(Luke 19:8)**. The good Samaritan helped his neighbor but the priest and Levite did not **(Luke 10:29–37)**.

The Eighth Commandment

[God's Gift of a Good Reputation]

You shall not give false testimony against your neighbor.

What does this mean? We should fear and love God so that we do not tell lies about our neighbor, betray him, slander him, or hurt his reputation, but defend him, speak well of him, and explain everything in the kindest way.

61. What does God forbid in the Eighth Commandment?

A. God forbids us to tell lies about our neighbor in a court of law or elsewhere, that is, to lie about, lie to, or withhold the truth from our neighbor.

203   **Prov. 19:5** A false witness will not go unpunished, and he who pours out lies will not go free.

204   **Eph. 4:25** Each of you must put off falsehood and speak truthfully to his neighbor, for we are all members of one body.

Bible narratives: False witnesses testified against Jesus **(Matt. 26:59–61).** False witnesses testified against

Naboth **(1 Kings 21:13)**. Gehazi lied about Elisha and then lied to him **(2 Kings 5:22–25)**.

B. God forbids us to betray our neighbor, that is, to reveal our neighbor's secrets.

205   **Prov. 11:13** A gossip betrays a confidence, but a trustworthy man keeps a secret.

Bible narratives: Doeg betrayed Ahimelech **(1 Sam. 22:6–19)**. Judas betrayed Jesus **(Matt. 26:14–16)**.

C. God forbids us to slander our neighbor or hurt our neighbor's reputation.

206   **Matt. 18:15** If your brother sins against you, go and show him his fault, just between the two of you.

207   **Luke 6:37** Do not judge, and you will not be judged. Do not condemn, and you will not be condemned.

208   **James 4:11** Brothers, do not slander one another.

Bible narrative: Absalom slandered his father **(2 Sam. 15:1–6)**.

62. What does God require of us in the Eighth Commandment?

A. We should defend our neighbor, that is, we should speak up for and protect our neighbor from false accusations.

209   **Prov. 31:8–9** Speak up for those who cannot speak for themselves, for the rights of all who are destitute. Speak up and judge fairly; defend the rights of the poor and needy.

B. We should speak well of our neighbor, that is, we should praise our neighbor's good actions and qualities.

Bible narratives: Jonathan spoke well of David **(1 Sam.**

19:4). The people of Capernaum spoke well of the centurion **(Luke 7:4–5).** Jesus spoke well of the woman who anointed Him **(Mark 14:3–9).**

C. We should put the best meaning on everything, that is, we should explain our neighbor's actions in the best possible way.

210   **1 Cor. 13:7** [Love] always protects, always trusts, always hopes, always perseveres.

211   **1 Peter 4:8** Love covers over a multitude of sins.

The Ninth Commandment

[God's Gift of Contentment]

You shall not covet your neighbor's house.

What does this mean? We should fear and love God so that we do not scheme to get our neighbor's inheritance or house, or get it in a way which only appears right, but help and be of service to him in keeping it.

63. What is coveting?

Coveting is having a sinful desire for anyone or anything that belongs to our neighbor.

212   **Rom. 7:8** Sin . . . produced in me every kind of covetous desire.

213   **Matt. 15:19** Out of the heart come evil thoughts, murder, adultery, sexual immorality, theft, false testimony, slander.

64. What coveting does God forbid in the Ninth Commandment?

God forbids every sinful desire to get our neighbor's possessions openly or by trickery.

214   **Micah 2:1–2** Woe to those who plan iniquity.
        . . . They covet fields and seize them, and houses, and
        take them. They defraud a man of his home, a
        fellowman of his inheritance.

215   **1 Tim. 6:8–10** If we have food and clothing, we will
        be content with that. People who want to get rich fall
        into temptation and a trap and into many foolish
        and harmful desires that plunge men into ruin and
        destruction. For the love of money is a root of all
        kinds of evil. Some people, eager for money, have
        wandered from the faith and pierced themselves
        with many griefs.

Bible narrative: Ahab coveted Naboth's vineyard and
got it in a way which only seemed right **(1 Kings 21:
1–16).**

*65. What does God require of us in the Ninth Com-
mandment?*

We should be content with what God has given us
and assist our neighbor in keeping what God has given
that person.

216   **Phil. 4:11** I am not saying this because I am in
        need, for I have learned to be content whatever the
        circumstances.

217   **1 Tim. 6:6** Godliness with contentment is great
        gain.

218   **Heb. 13:5** Keep your lives free from the love of
        money and be content with what you have, because
        God has said, "Never will I leave you; never will I
        forsake you."

Bible narrative: Paul overcame coveting **(Acts 20:
32–35).**

The Tenth Commandment

[God's Gift of Contentment]

You shall not covet your neighbor's wife, or his manservant or maidservant, his ox or donkey, or anything that belongs to your neighbor.

What does this mean? We should fear and love God so that we do not entice or force away our neighbor's wife, workers, or animals, or turn them against him, but urge them to stay and do their duty.

66. What coveting does God forbid in the Tenth Commandment?

God forbids every sinful desire to take from our neighbor that person's spouse or workers.

219   **Luke 12:15** He said to them, "Watch out! Be on your guard against all kinds of greed; a man's life does not consist in the abundance of his possessions."

220   **Col. 3:5** Put to death, therefore, whatever belongs to your earthly nature: sexual immorality, impurity, lust, evil desires and greed, which is idolatry.

Bible narratives: David coveted Uriah's wife and took her **(2 Sam. 11:2–4).** Absalom estranged the hearts of the people from David **(2 Sam. 15:1–6).**

67. What does God require of us in the Tenth Commandment?

We should be content with the helpers God has given us and encourage our neighbor's helpers to be faithful to our neighbor.

221   **Phil. 2:4** Each of you should look not only to your
       own interests, but also to the interests of others.

Bible narrative: Paul returned a runaway slave to his
master Philemon **(Philemon).**

*68. What does God particularly impress upon us in
the last two commandments?*

A. In God's sight evil desire, coveting, is indeed sin
and deserves condemnation.

222   **Gen. 3:6** When the woman saw that the fruit of the
       tree was good for food and pleasing to the eye, and
       also desirable for gaining wisdom, she took some
       and ate it.

223   **James 1:14–15** Each one is tempted when, by his
       own evil desire, he is dragged away and enticed.
       Then, after desire has conceived, it gives birth to sin;
       and sin, when it is full-grown, gives birth to death.

B. God wants us to love Him and to have holy
desires.

224   **Ps. 37:4** Delight yourself in the Lord and He will
       give you the desires of your heart.

225   **Ps. 119:35–36** Direct me in the path of Your
       commands, for there I find delight. Turn my heart
       toward Your statutes and not toward selfish gain.

226   **Phil. 4:8** Finally, brothers, whatever is true, what-
       ever is noble, whatever is right, whatever is pure,
       whatever is lovely, whatever is admirable—if
       anything is excellent or praiseworthy—think about
       such things.

The Close of the Commandments

What does God say about all these commandments? He says: "I, the Lord your God, am a jealous God, punishing the children for the sin of the fathers to the third and fourth generation of those who hate Me, but showing love to a thousand generations of those who love Me and keep My commandments." **[Ex. 20:5–6]**

What does this mean? God threatens to punish all who break these commandments. Therefore, we should fear His wrath and not do anything against them. But He promises grace and every blessing to all who keep these commandments. Therefore, we should also love and trust in Him and gladly do what He commands.

69. *Why does God call Himself a jealous God?*

Because God is holy

A. He hates sin and insists on strict and perfect obedience;

B. He will not share with idols the love and honor we owe Him;

C. He will punish those who hate Him.

227   **Ps. 5:4–5** You are not a God who takes pleasure in evil; with You the wicked cannot dwell. The arrogant cannot stand in Your presence; You hate all who do wrong.

228   **Is. 42:8** I am the Lord; that is My name! I will not give My glory to another or My praise to idols.

229   **Ezek. 6:9** I have been grieved by their adulterous hearts, which have turned away from Me, and by their eyes, which have lusted after their idols.

230   **James 4:12** There is only one Lawgiver and Judge, the one who is able to save and destroy.

70. What does God threaten to do to all who hate Him and break His commandments?

God threatens earthly punishment, physical death, and eternal damnation.

231   **Lev. 26:18** If after all this you will not listen to Me, I will punish you for your sins seven times over.

232   **Rom. 6:23** The wages of sin is death.

233   **Gal. 3:10** Cursed is everyone who does not continue to do everything written in the Book of the Law.

71. What does God mean when He threatens to punish the children for the sin of the fathers to the third and fourth generation of those who hate Him?

If the children, grandchildren, and great-grandchildren also hate God and follow in the evil ways of their parents, then God will during their earthly lives punish them for the sins of their ancestors.

234   **Ezek. 18:20** The soul who sins is the one who will die. The son will not share the guilt of the father, nor will the father share the guilt of the son. The righteousness of the righteous man will be credited to him, and the wickedness of the wicked will be charged against him.

Bible narratives: The family of wicked Ahab and Jezebel were destroyed **(2 Kings 9:7–8; 10:11).** Israel was led into captivity for its disobedience and wickedness **(2 Chron. 36:17–21).**

72. Why does God threaten such punishment?

God threatens such punishment to make us fear His anger, so that we do not act against His commandments.

235   **Eccl. 12:13–14** Fear God and keep His commandments, for this is the whole duty of man. For God will bring every deed into judgment, including every hidden thing, whether it is good or evil.

236   **Matt. 10:28** Do not be afraid of those who kill the body but cannot kill the soul. Rather, be afraid of the One who can destroy both soul and body in hell.

73. How does God bless those who love Him and keep His commandments?

He showers those who believe in Him and their God-fearing descendants with His constant love and good gifts.

237   **1 Tim. 4:8** Godliness has value for all things, holding promise for both the present life and the life to come.

Bible narrative: God blessed Job for his faithfulness **(Job 42:10–17).**

The Fulfillment of the Law

74. How carefully does God want us to keep His commandments?

God wants us to keep His commandments perfectly in thoughts, desires, words, and deeds.

238   **Lev. 19:2** Be holy because I, the Lord your God, am holy.

239   **James 2:10** Whoever keeps the whole law and yet stumbles at just one point is guilty of breaking all of it.

75. What prevents us from keeping God's commandments perfectly?

Our sinful nature makes it impossible.

240   **Ps. 14:3** All have turned aside, they have together become corrupt; there is no one who does good, not even one.

241   **Eccl. 7:20** There is not a righteous man on earth who does what is right and never sins.

242   **Is. 64:6** All of us have become like one who is unclean, and all our righteous acts are like filthy rags.

243   **1 John 1:8** If we claim to be without sin, we deceive ourselves and the truth is not in us.

Bible narrative: The apostle Paul grieved over his failure to keep the Law **(Rom. 7:15–20).**

76. Can anyone, then, be saved by the Law?

No; the Law condemns everyone.

244   **Gal. 3:10–11** All who rely on observing the law are under a curse, for it is written: "Cursed is everyone who does not continue to do everything written in the Book of the Law." Clearly no one is justified before God by the law.

The Purposes of the Law

77. What purposes does the Law then serve?

A. First, the Law helps to control violent outbursts of sin and keeps order in the world (a curb).

245   **1 Tim. 1:9** We also know that law is made not for the righteous [good people] but for lawbreakers and rebels, the ungodly and sinful, the unholy and irreligious; for those who kill their fathers or mothers.

246   **Rom. 2:14–15** Indeed, when Gentiles, who do not have the law, do by nature things required by the law, they are a law for themselves, even though they do not have the law, since they show that the requirements of the law are written on their hearts, their consciences also bearing witness, and their thoughts now accusing, now even defending them.

B. Second, the Law accuses us and shows us our sin (a mirror).

247   **Rom. 3:20** Through the law we become conscious of sin.

248   **Rom. 7:7** I would not have known what coveting really was if the law had not said, "Do not covet."

C. Third, the Law teaches us Christians what we should and should not do to lead a God-pleasing life (a guide). The power to live according to the Law comes from the Gospel.

249   **Ps. 119:9** How can a young man keep his way pure? By living according to Your word.

250   **Ps. 119:105** Your word is a lamp to my feet and a light for my path.

251   **1 John 4:9, 11** This is how God showed His love among us: He sent His one and only Son into the world that we might live through Him. . . . Dear friends, since God so loved us, we also ought to love one another.

Note: See **Luke 10:27.**

Sin

78. What is sin?

Sin is every thought, desire, word, and deed which is contrary to God's Law.

252   **1 John 3:4** Everyone who sins breaks the law; in fact, sin is lawlessness.

Note: Other names for sin are *disobedience* (**Rom. 5:19**); *debts* (**Matt. 6:12**); *wickedness, rebellion* (**Ex. 34:7**); *fault* (**Matt. 18:15**); *trespass* (**Rom. 5:17**); *wickedness* (**Rom. 6:13**); and *wrong* (**Col. 3:25**).

79. Who brought sin into the world?

The devil brought sin into the world by tempting Adam and Eve, who of their own free will yielded to the temptation.

253   **1 John 3:8** He who does what is sinful is of the devil, because the devil has been sinning from the beginning.

254   **Rom. 5:12** Sin entered the world through one man.

Bible narrative: The fall of humanity (**Gen. 3:1–7**).

80. How many kinds of sin are there?

There are two kinds of sin: original sin and actual sin.

81. What is original sin?

Original sin is that total corruption of our whole human nature which we have inherited from Adam through our parents.

255   **Ps. 51:5** I was sinful at birth, sinful from the time my mother conceived me.

256   **John 3:6** Flesh gives birth to flesh, but the Spirit gives birth to spirit.

257   **Rom. 5:12** Sin entered the world through one man, and death through sin, and in this way death came to all men, because all sinned.

258   **Eph. 4:22** Put off, concerning your former conduct, the old man which grows corrupt according to the deceitful lusts (NKJV).

82. What has original sin done to human nature?

Original sin

A. has brought guilt and condemnation to all people;

259   **Rom. 5:19** Through the disobedience of the one man the many were made sinners.

260   **Eph. 2:3** Like the rest, we were by nature objects of wrath.

B. has left everyone without true fear and love of God, that is, spiritually blind, dead, and enemies of God;

261   **Gen. 8:21** Every inclination of his [man's] heart is evil from childhood.

262   **1 Cor. 2:14** The man without the Spirit does not accept the things that come from the Spirit of God, for they are foolishness to him, and he cannot understand them, because they are spiritually discerned.

263   **Eph. 2:1** As for you, you were dead in your transgressions and sins.

264   **Rom. 8:7** The sinful mind is hostile to God. It does not submit to God's law, nor can it do so.

C. causes everyone to commit all kinds of actual sins.

265   **Matt. 7:17** Every good tree bears good fruit, but a bad tree bears bad fruit.

266   **Gal. 5:19** The acts of the sinful nature are obvious: sexual immorality, impurity and debauchery; idolatry and witchcraft; hatred, discord, jealousy, fits of rage, selfish ambition, dissensions, factions and envy; drunkenness, orgies, and the like.

83. What is actual sin?

Actual sin is every act against a commandment of God in thoughts, desires, words, or deeds.

267   **Matt. 15:19** Out of the heart come evil thoughts, murder, adultery, sexual immorality, theft, false testimony, slander.

268   **James 1:15** After desire has conceived, it gives birth to sin. (Sins of commission)

269   **James 4:17** Anyone, then, who knows the good he ought to do and doesn't do it, sins. (Sins of omission)

Law and Gospel

84. Where alone does God offer the forgiveness of sins?

God offers the forgiveness of sins only in the Gospel, the good news that we are freed from the guilt, the punishment, and the power of sin, and are saved eternally because of Christ's keeping the Law and His suffering and death for us.

270   **John 3:16** God so loved the world that He gave His one and only Son, that whoever believes in Him shall not perish but have eternal life.

271   **Rom. 1:16** I am not ashamed of the gospel, because it is the power of God for the salvation of everyone who believes.

272   **Rom. 10:4** Christ is the end of the law so that there may be righteousness for everyone who believes.

273   **Gal. 3:13** Christ redeemed us from the curse of the law by becoming a curse for us, for it is written: "Cursed is everyone who is hung on a tree."

274   **Col. 1:13–14** He has rescued us from the dominion of darkness and brought us into the kingdom of the Son He loves, in whom we have redemption, the forgiveness of sins.

85. What is the difference between the Law and the Gospel?

A. The Law teaches what we are to do and not to do; the Gospel teaches what God has done, and still does, for our salvation.

B. The Law shows us our sin and the wrath of God; the Gospel shows us our Savior and the grace of God.

C. The Law must be proclaimed to all people, but especially to impenitent sinners; the Gospel must be proclaimed to sinners who are troubled in their minds because of their sins.

THE APOSTLES' CREED

86. What is a creed?

A creed is a statement of what we believe, teach, and confess.

275   **Rom. 10:10** It is with your heart that you believe and are justified, and it is with your mouth that you confess and are saved.

I Believe

87. What is meant by "I believe in God"?

It means I trust God and His promises and accept as true all He teaches in the Holy Scriptures.

276   **Ps. 31:14** I trust in You, O Lord; I say, "You are my God."

277   **Ps. 37:5** Commit your way to the Lord; trust in Him.

278   **Rom. 10:17** Faith comes from hearing the message, and the message is heard through the word of Christ.

279   **Heb. 11:1** Faith is being sure of what we hope for and certain of what we do not see.

88. Why do we say, "I believe," and not, "We believe"?

Everyone must believe for himself or herself, no one can be saved by another's faith.

280   **Hab. 2:4** The righteous will live by his faith.

281   **Luke 7:50** Your faith has saved you; go in peace.

Bible narrative: The foolish virgins could not obtain oil from the wise virgins **(Matt. 25:1–13).**

89. What three creeds are used by the church?

The Apostles', the Nicene, and the Athanasian.

90. Which creed is used in Luther's Catechism?

The Apostles' Creed.

91. Why is it called the Apostles' Creed?

It is called the Apostles' Creed, not because it was written by the apostles themselves, but because it states briefly the doctrine (teaching) which God gave through the apostles in the Bible. The Creed is trinitarian because the Scriptures reveal God as triune. Christians are baptized in the name of the triune God: Father, Son, and Holy Spirit.

282   **Matt. 28:19** Go and make disciples of all nations, baptizing them in the name of the Father and of the Son and of the Holy Spirit.

283   **Eph. 4:4–6** There is one body and one Spirit—just as you were called to one hope when you were called—one Lord, one faith, one baptism; one God and Father of all, who is over all and through all and in all.

92. In what ways does the triune God make Himself known?

A. Through the existence of the world (natural knowledge of God).

284   **Ps. 19:1** The heavens declare the glory of God; the skies declare the work of His hands.

285   **Rom. 1:19–20** What may be known about God is plain to them, because God has made it plain to them. For since the creation of the world God's invisible qualities—His eternal power and divine nature—have been clearly seen, being understood from what has been made, so that men are without excuse.

286   **Heb. 3:4** Every house is built by someone, but God is the builder of everything.

B. Through conscience (natural knowledge of God).

287   **Rom. 2:15** They show that the requirements of the law are written on their hearts, their consciences also bearing witness, and their thoughts now accusing, now even defending them.

C. Especially through the Holy Scriptures in which God clearly reveals Himself and His gift of salvation in Christ (revealed knowledge of God).

288   **John 20:31** These [acts of Jesus] are written that You may believe that Jesus is the Christ, the Son of God, and that by believing you may have life in His name.

289   **2 Tim. 3:15** From infancy you have known the holy Scriptures, which are able to make you wise for salvation through faith in Christ Jesus.

290   **Heb. 1:1–2** In the past God spoke to our forefathers through the prophets at many times and in various ways, but in these last days He has spoken to us by His Son, whom He appointed heir of all things, and through whom He made the universe.

93. Who is God?

In His Word God has told us that He is

A. spirit (a personal being without a body);

291   **John 4:24** God is spirit.

B. eternal (without beginning and without end);

292   **Ps. 90:1–2** Lord, You have been our dwelling place throughout all generations. Before the mountains were born or You brought forth the earth and the world, from everlasting to everlasting You are God.

293   **1 Tim. 1:17** To the King eternal, immortal, invisible, the only God, be honor and glory for ever and ever. Amen.

C. unchangeable (immutable);

294   **Ps. 102:27** You remain the same, and Your years will never end.

295   **Mal. 3:6** I the Lord do not change.

296   **James 1:17** Every good and perfect gift is from above, coming down from the Father of the heavenly lights, who does not change like shifting shadows.

D. almighty, all-powerful (omnipotent);

297   **Gen. 17:1** I am God Almighty.

298   **Matt. 19:26** With God all things are possible.

E. all-knowing (omniscient);

299 **Ps. 139:1–4** O Lord, You have searched me and You know me. You know when I sit and when I rise; You perceive my thoughts from afar. You discern my going out and my lying down; You are familiar with all my ways. Before a word is on my tongue You know it completely, O Lord.

300 **John 21:17** Lord, You know all things.

F. present everywhere (omnipresent);

301 **Jer. 23:24** "Can anyone hide in secret places so that I cannot see him?" declares the Lord. "Do not I fill heaven and earth?" declares the Lord.

302 **Acts 17:27** He is not far from each one of us.

G. holy (sinless and hating sin);

303 **Lev. 19:2** I, the Lord your God, am holy.

304 **Ps. 5:4–5** You are not a God who takes pleasure in evil; with You the wicked cannot dwell. The arrogant cannot stand in Your presence; You hate all who do wrong.

305 **Is. 6:3** Holy, holy, holy is the Lord Almighty.

H. just (fair and impartial);

306 **Deut. 32:4** He is the Rock, His works are perfect, and all His ways are just. A faithful God who does no wrong, upright and just is He.

I. faithful (keeping His promises);

307 **2 Tim. 2:13** If we are faithless, He will remain faithful, for He cannot disown Himself.

J. good (kind, desiring our welfare);

308 **Ps. 118:1** Give thanks to the Lord, for He is good; His love endures forever.

309 **Ps. 145:9** The Lord is good to all; He has compassion on all He has made.

K. merciful (full of pity);

310   **Jer. 3:12** "I am merciful," declares the Lord.
311   **Titus 3:5** He saved us, not because of righteous things we had done, but because of His mercy.

L. gracious (showing undeserved kindness, forgiving);

312   **Ex. 34:6–7** The Lord, the Lord, the compassionate and gracious God, slow to anger, abounding in love and faithfulness, maintaining love to thousands, and forgiving wickedness, rebellion and sin.

M. love.

313   **John 3:16** God so loved the world that He gave His one and only Son, that whoever believes in Him shall not perish but have eternal life.
314   **1 John 4:8** God is love.

Note: God's attributes tell us what God is. God is each of these, all of these, and more than these attributes.

94. Who is the only true God?

The only true God is the triune God: Father, Son, and Holy Spirit, three distinct persons in one divine being (the Holy Trinity).

95. How are the three divine persons distinguished from each other?

The Father has begotten the Son from eternity; the Son is begotten of the Father from eternity; the Holy Spirit from eternity proceeds from the Father and the Son. To the Father especially is ascribed the work of creation; to the Son, the work of redemption; to the Holy Spirit, the work of sanctification.

315   **Ps. 2:7** You are My Son; today I have become Your Father.

316   **John 15:26** When the Counselor comes, whom I will send to you from the Father, the Spirit of truth who goes out from the Father, He will testify about Me.

317   **Gal. 4:6** Because you are sons, God sent the Spirit of His Son into our hearts, the Spirit who calls out, "*Abba,* Father."

The First Article

Creation

I believe in God, the Father Almighty, Maker of heaven and earth.

What does this mean? I believe that God has made me and all creatures; that He has given me my body and soul, eyes, ears, and all my members, my reason and all my senses, and still takes care of them.

He also gives me clothing and shoes, food and drink, house and home, wife and children, land, animals, and all I have. He richly and daily provides me with all that I need to support this body and life.

He defends me against all danger and guards and protects me from all evil.

All this He does only out of fatherly, divine goodness and mercy, without any merit or worthiness in me. For all this it is my duty to thank and praise, serve and obey Him.

This is most certainly true.

96. Why is the first person of the Trinity called "the Father"?

A. God is the Father of my Lord Jesus Christ and also my Father through faith in Christ.

318   **Matt. 3:17** A voice from heaven said, "This is My Son, whom I love; with Him I am well pleased."

319   **John 20:17** I am returning to My Father and your Father, to My God and your God.

320   **Gal. 3:26** You are all sons of God through faith in Christ Jesus.

B. He is also the Father of all people because He created them. Strictly speaking, there is only one human race, because all human beings are equally the children of Adam and Eve and are equally redeemed by Christ.

321   **Mal. 2:10** Have we not all one Father? Did not one God create us?

322   **Acts 17:26** From one man He made every nation of men, that they should inhabit the whole earth.

323   **1 Cor. 15:22** As in Adam all die, so in Christ all will be made alive.

324   **Eph. 3:14–15** For this reason I kneel before the Father, from whom His whole family in heaven and on earth derives its name.

Bible narrative: The prodigal son **(Luke 15:11–32).**

God Made Me and All Creatures

97. Why is God, the Father Almighty called "Maker of heaven and earth"?

Because in six days He created all things, out of nothing, simply by His word.

325   **Gen. 1:1** In the beginning God created the heavens and the earth.

326   **Ps. 33:6, 9** By the word of the Lord were the heavens made, their starry host by the breath of His mouth. . . . For He spoke, and it came to be; He commanded, and it stood firm.

327   **Heb. 11:3** By faith we understand that the universe was formed at God's command, so that what is seen was not made out of what was visible.

Bible narrative: Creation **(Genesis 1–2).**

98. What is meant by "heaven and earth"?

All things visible and invisible.

328   **Col. 1:16** By Him all things were created: things in heaven and on earth, visible and invisible.

The Angels

99. Which invisible beings created by God are especially important to us?

The angels.

Note: Angel means "messenger." God frequently used angels to announce important events in the history of salvation: the birth of John the Baptist **(Luke 1:1–20);** the birth of Jesus **(Luke 1:26–38; Matt. 1:18–21);** the resurrection of Jesus **(Luke 24:4–7);** the ascension and second coming of Jesus **(Acts 1:10–11).**

100. What else does the Bible tell us about angels?

A. They are spirit beings who were created holy.

329   **Gen. 1:31** God saw all that He had made, and it was very good. And there was evening, and there was morning—the sixth day.

B. Some angels rebelled against God. They are the devils or demons.

330   **2 Peter 2:4** God did not spare angels when they sinned, but sent them to hell, putting them into gloomy dungeons to be held for judgment.

C. The good angels are many and powerful. They serve God and help us.

331   **Dan. 7:10** Thousands upon thousands attended Him; ten thousand times ten thousand stood before Him.

332   **Luke 2:13** Suddenly a great company of the heavenly host appeared with the angel, praising God.

333   **Ps. 103:20–21** Praise the Lord, you His angels, you mighty ones who do His bidding, who obey His word. Praise the Lord, all His heavenly hosts, you His servants who do His will.

334   **Ps. 91:11–12** He will command His angels concerning you to guard you in all your ways; they will lift you up in their hands so that you will not strike your foot against a stone.

335   **Heb. 1:14** Are not all angels ministering spirits sent to serve those who will inherit salvation?

Bible narratives: One angel put to death 185,000 of Sennacherib's army **(2 Kings 19:35).** Elisha and his servant were protected by the heavenly hosts **(2 Kings 6:15–17).** An angel set Peter free **(Acts 12:5–11).**

D. The evil angels are also many and powerful. They hate God and seek to destroy everything that is good, especially faith in Christ.

336   **Mark 5:9** Jesus asked him, "What is your name?" "My name is Legion," he replied, "for we are many."

337   **Eph. 6:12** Our struggle is not against flesh and blood, but against the rulers, against the authorities, against the powers of this dark world and against the spiritual forces of evil in the heavenly realms.

338   **Mark 4:15** Some people are like seed along the path, where the word is sown. As soon as they hear it, Satan comes along and takes away the word that was sown in them.

339   **John 8:44** You belong to your father, the devil, and you want to carry out your father's desire. He was a murderer from the beginning, not holding to the truth, for there is no truth in him. When he lies, he speaks his native language, for he is a liar and the father of lies.

340   **1 Peter 5:8–9** Be self-controlled and alert. Your enemy the devil prowls around like a roaring lion looking for someone to devour. Resist him, standing firm in the faith, because you know that your brothers throughout the world are undergoing the same kind of sufferings.

Bible narratives: The serpent led Eve into sin **(Gen. 3:1–5)**. Satan sought the destruction of Job **(Job 2)**. The tempter tried to mislead Jesus **(Matt. 4:1–11)**.

Humanity

101. Who are human beings?

Human beings are the most important visible creatures. God created Adam and Eve in His own image, with authority over all the earth.

341   **Gen. 2:7** The Lord God formed man from the dust of the ground and breathed into his nostrils the breath of life, and the man became a living being.

342   **Gen. 1:26–28** God said, "Let Us make man in Our
       image, in Our likeness, and let them rule over the
       fish of the sea and the birds of the air, over the live-
       stock, over all the earth, and over all the creatures
       that move along the ground." So God created man in
       His own image, in the image of God He created him;
       male and female He created them. God blessed them
       and said to them, "Be fruitful and increase in
       number; fill the earth and subdue it. Rule over the
       fish of the sea and the birds of the air and over every
       living creature that moves on the ground."

343   **Mark 10:6** [Jesus said] "At the beginning of creation
       God 'made them male and female.'"

102. Why do we say, "God has made me"?

God created the first man and woman, and God has
created each one of us.

344   **Gen. 1:28** God blessed them and said to them, "Be
       fruitful and increase in number; fill the earth and
       subdue it. Rule over the fish of the sea and the birds
       of the air and over every living creature that moves
       on the ground."

345   **Ps. 139:13** You created my inmost being; You knit
       me together in my mother's womb.

346   **Jer. 1:5** Before I formed you in the womb I knew
       you.

103. How did God first create life?

God created all living things, both plant and animal,
by His Word alone, from nothing. He created humanity
specially, from dust, then gave us His own breath as life.

347   **Gen. 2:7** The Lord God formed the man from the
       dust of the ground and breathed into his nostrils the
       breath of life, and the man became a living being.

348   **Ps. 139:14** I praise You because I am fearfully and
         wonderfully made; Your works are wonderful, I
         know that full well.

104. What plan does God use for the reproduction of living things?

God created living things to reproduce "according to
their kinds." Animals, plants, and people can reproduce
only living things like themselves.

349   **Gen. 1:21** God created the great creatures of the sea
         and every living and moving thing with which the
         water teems, according to their kinds, and every
         winged bird according to its kind. And God saw that
         it was good.

350   **Gen. 1:24** God said, "Let the land produce living
         creatures according to their kinds: livestock, crea-
         tures that move along the ground, and wild animals,
         each according to its kind."

105. What is the Christian's proper response to theories of evolution regarding the beginning of the world?

By faith Christians believe what the Word of God
teaches about creation. Evolutionary theories are not
scientifically verifiable.

351   **Heb. 11:3** By faith we understand that the universe
         was formed at God's command, so that what is seen
         was not made out of what was visible.

352   **2 Peter 3:5–6** They deliberately forget that long ago
         by God's word the heavens existed and the earth was
         formed out of water and by water. By these waters
         also the world of that time was deluged and
         destroyed.

353   **1 Tim. 6:20–21** Guard what has been entrusted to
         your care. Turn away from godless chatter and the

opposing ideas of what is falsely called knowledge, which some have professed and in so doing have wandered from the faith.

106. What was the image of God?

The image of God was this:

A. Adam and Eve truly knew God as He wishes to be known and were perfectly happy in Him.

354   **Col. 3:10** Put on the new man who is renewed in knowledge according to the image of Him who created him (NKJV).

B. They were righteous and holy, doing God's will.

355   **Eph. 4:24** Put on the new man which was created according to God, in righteousness and true holiness (NKJV).

107. Do people still have the image of God?

No, this image was lost when our first parents disobeyed God and fell into sin. Their will and intellect lost the ability to know and please God. In Christians God has begun to rebuild His image, but only in heaven will it be fully restored.

356   **Gen. 3:8–10** The man and his wife heard the sound of the Lord God as He was walking in the garden in the cool of the day, and they hid from the Lord God among the trees of the garden. But the Lord God called to the man, "Where are you?" He answered, "I heard You in the garden, and I was afraid because I was naked; so I hid."

357   **Gen. 5:3** [Adam] had a son in his own likeness, in his own image.

358   **1 Cor. 2:14** The man without the Spirit does not accept the things that come from the Spirit of God,

for they are foolishness to him, and he cannot understand them, because they are spiritually discerned.

359   **Ps. 17:15** In righteousness I will see Your face; when I awake, I will be satisfied with seeing Your likeness.

God Still Takes Care of Me and All Creatures

108. How does the universe still depend on God?

God sustains all things by His wisdom and power.

360   **Ps. 36:6** O Lord, You preserve both man and beast.
361   **Ps. 147:4** He determines the number of the stars and calls them each by name.
362   **Heb. 1:3** The Son is the radiance of God's glory and the exact representation of His being, sustaining all things by His powerful word.
363   **Col. 1:17** [Jesus] is before all things, and in Him all things hold together.

109. Why are there evil and suffering in this world?

Evil and suffering are in the world because of sin. But in the suffering, death, and resurrection of Jesus Christ, God has demonstrated His power over sin and death. God in His almighty power and love causes all things to work together for good to those who love Him.

364   **Rom. 6:23** The wages of sin is death, but the gift of God is eternal life in Christ Jesus our Lord.
365   **Rom. 8:28** We know that in all things God works for the good of those who love Him, who have been called according to His purpose.

366   **Rom. 8:37** In all these things we are more than conquerors through Him who loved us.

110. What does God do to take care of me?

A. He gives me food and clothing, home and family, work and play, and all that I need from day to day.

367   **Ps. 145:15–16** The eyes of all look to You, and You give them their food at the proper time. You open Your hand and satisfy the desires of every living thing.

368   **1 Peter 5:7** Cast all your anxiety on Him because He cares for you.

Bible narratives: God took care of Noah and his descendants **(Gen. 9:1–3).** God took care of Israel in the wilderness **(Deut. 8:3–4).** God took care of Elijah, the widow, and her son during the famine **(1 Kings 17).** See **Psalms 37** and **104.**

B. "He defends me against all danger and guards and protects me from all evil."

369   **Gen. 50:20** You intended to harm me, but God intended it for good to accomplish what is now being done, the saving of many lives.

370   **Ps. 31:15** My times are in Your hands.

371   **Matt. 10:29–30** Are not two sparrows sold for a penny? Yet not one of them will fall to the ground apart from the will of your Father. And even the very hairs of your head are all numbered.

Bible narratives: God directed Lot to flee to the mountains before the destruction of Sodom **(Genesis 19).** God delivered Israel from slavery and guided and protected them on their way **(Ex. 13:14).** See also **Psalms 37** and **73.**

111. Why does God do this for us?

"All this He does only out of fatherly, divine goodness and mercy, without any merit or worthiness in me."

372   **Gen. 32:10** I am unworthy of all the kindness and faithfulness You have shown Your servant.

373   **Ps. 103:13** As a father has compassion on his children, so the Lord has compassion on those who fear Him.

Bible narrative: The centurion of Capernaum confessed that he did not deserve to have the Lord come under his roof **(Luke 7:6–7).**

112. What do we owe our heavenly Father for all His goodness?

It is our duty to

A. "Thank and praise, serve and obey Him";

374   **Ps. 116:12** How can I repay the Lord for all His goodness to me?

375   **Ps. 118:1** Give thanks to the Lord, for He is good; His love endures forever.

B. be good stewards of His creation.

376   **Gen. 2:15** The Lord God took the man and put him in the Garden of Eden to work it and take care of it.

Note: We are good stewards when we avoid polluting air, land, and water; carefully dispose of waste; use rather than waste natural resources; conserve rather than waste energy; recycle or reuse materials whenever possible; and value and take care of all God's creation.

113. Why do we close the explanation of the First Article with the words, "This is most certainly true"?

Everything I confess in this article is plainly taught in God's Word, Holy Scripture. Therefore, I firmly believe it.

The Second Article

Redemption

[I believe] in Jesus Christ, His only Son, our Lord, who was conceived by the Holy Spirit, born of the Virgin Mary, suffered under Pontius Pilate, was crucified, died and was buried. He descended into hell. The third day He rose again from the dead. He ascended into heaven and sits at the right hand of God, the Father Almighty. From thence He will come to judge the living and the dead.

What does this mean? I believe that Jesus Christ, true God, begotten of the Father from eternity, and also true man, born of the Virgin Mary, is my Lord,

who has redeemed me, a lost and condemned person, purchased and won me from all sins, from death, and from the power of the devil; not with gold or silver, but with His holy, precious blood and with His innocent suffering and death,

that I may be His own and live under Him in His kingdom and serve Him in everlasting righteousness, innocence, and blessedness,

just as He is risen from the dead, lives and reigns to all eternity.

This is most certainly true.

The Names *Jesus* and *Christ*

114. Of whom does this article speak?

It speaks about Jesus Christ—His person and His work.

115. Why is He named Jesus?

The name *Jesus* means "the Lord saves." Jesus is His personal name.

377   **Matt. 1:21** She will give birth to a son, and you are to give Him the name Jesus, because He will save His people from their sins.

378   **John 4:42** We know that this man really is the Savior of the world.

379   **Acts 4:12** Salvation is found in no one else, for there is no other name under heaven given to men by which we must be saved.

116. Why is He called Christ?

The title *Christ* (Greek) or *Messiah* (Hebrew) means "the Anointed." Jesus has been anointed with the Holy Spirit without limit to be our Prophet, Priest, and King.

Note: Anointing was the way prophets, priests, and kings were set apart for special work.

380   **Ps. 45:7** God, your God, has set you above your companions by anointing you with the oil of joy.

381   **John 3:34** The one whom God has sent speaks the words of God, for God gives the Spirit without limit.

382   **Acts 10:38** God anointed Jesus of Nazareth with the Holy Spirit and power.

Note: The following are other titles for Jesus: Angel of God **(Ex. 14:19)**; Redeemer **(Is. 59:20)**; Immanuel **(Matt. 1:23)**; Son of the living God **(Matt. 16:16)**;

Son of Man **(Matt. 25:31)**; the Word **(John 1:14)**; Lord **(John 20:28)**. His names are the Gospel simply stated.

117. What does it mean when you confess, "I believe in Jesus Christ"?

It means that I know and trust in Jesus Christ as my only Savior from sin, death, and the devil and believe that He gives me eternal life.

383   **John 17:3** This is eternal life: that they may know You, the only true God, and Jesus Christ, whom You have sent.

384   **John 3:36** Whoever believes in the Son has eternal life, but whoever rejects the Son will not see life, for God's wrath remains on him.

385   **2 Tim. 1:12** I know whom I have believed, and am convinced that He is able to guard what I have entrusted to Him for that day.

386   **Rom. 10:10** It is with your heart that you believe and are justified, and it is with your mouth that you confess and are saved.

The Two Natures of Jesus Christ

118. Who is Jesus Christ?

Jesus Christ is "true God, begotten of the Father from eternity, and also true man, born of the Virgin Mary."

119. How do you know that Jesus Christ is true God?

Because the Scriptures clearly call Him God, teaching the following:

A. Jesus has divine names.

387   **John 20:28** Thomas said to Him, "My Lord and my God!"

388   **Rom. 9:5** From them is traced the human ancestry of Christ, who is God over all, forever praised!

389   **1 John 5:20** He is the true God and eternal life.

Note: These names are not mere honorary titles but tell exactly who Jesus is, and they can be true only of God.

B. Jesus possesses divine attributes (qualities or characteristics). He is

1. eternal (without beginning and without end);

390   **John 1:1–2** In the beginning was the Word, and the Word was with God, and the Word was God. He was with God in the beginning.

2. unchangeable;

391   **Heb. 13:8** Jesus Christ is the same yesterday and today and forever.

3. almighty (omnipotent);

392   **Matt. 28:18** All authority in heaven and on earth has been given to Me.

4. all-knowing (omniscient);

393   **John 21:17** Lord, You know all things.

5. present everywhere (omnipresent).

394   **Matt. 28:20** Surely I am with you always, to the very end of the age.

Bible narratives: Miraculous catch of fish **(Luke 5:4–6; John 21:6).** Jesus knows the name and character of Nathanael **(John 1:48).** Jesus and the woman at Jacob's well **(John 4:17–18).**

Note: See also **Matt. 21:1–7; 26:20–25; Luke 18:31–33; 22:8–13.**

C. Jesus does divine works (which only God can do).

1. He forgives.

395 **Matt. 9:6** The Son of Man has authority on earth to forgive sins.

2. He created.

396 **John 1:3** Through Him all things were made; without Him nothing was made that has been made.

3. He will judge.

397 **John 5:27** [The Father] has given Him authority to judge.

4. He preserves.

398 **Heb. 1:3** [He sustains] all things by His powerful word.

Bible narratives: At the wedding feast in Cana, Jesus revealed His glory by turning water into wine **(John 2:1–11).** He rebuked the storm **(Luke 8:22–25).** He healed the paralytic **(Matt. 9:1–8).** He called Lazarus back to life **(John 11:38–44).** He rose from the dead **(Matt. 28:6–7).**

D. Jesus receives divine honor and glory.

399 **John 5:22–23** The Father judges no one, but has entrusted all judgment to the Son, that all may honor the Son just as they honor the Father. He who does not honor the Son does not honor the Father, who sent Him.

400 **Heb. 1:6** Let all God's angels worship Him.

Note: See **Phil. 2:10; Rev. 5:12–13.**

120. How do you know that Jesus Christ is also true man?

Because the Scriptures

A. clearly call Him man;

401   **1 Tim. 2:5** There is one God and one mediator between God and men, the man Christ Jesus.

B. say that He has a human body and soul;

402   **Luke 24:39** Look at My hands and My feet. It is I Myself. Touch Me and see; a ghost does not have flesh and bones, as you see I have.

403   **Matt. 26:38** My soul is overwhelmed with sorrow to the point of death.

C. speak of His human, but sinless, feelings and actions.

404   **Matt. 4:2** He was hungry.

405   **John 11:35** Jesus wept.

406   **John 19:28** Jesus said, "I am thirsty."

407   **Heb. 4:14–16** Since we have a great high priest who has gone through the heavens, Jesus the Son of God, let us hold firmly to the faith we profess. For we do not have a high priest who is unable to sympathize with our weaknesses, but we have one who has been tempted in every way, just as we are—yet was without sin. Let us then approach the throne of grace with confidence, so that we may receive mercy and find grace to help us in our time of need.

Bible narratives: Jesus suffered and died **(Matthew 26–27)**. Jesus slept **(Mark 4:38)**. Jesus was born **(Luke 2)**.

121. What two natures, therefore, are united in the one person of Jesus Christ?

The divine and the human natures are united in Jesus Christ. This personal union began when He became man (incarnation) and continues forever.

408   **John 1:14** The Word became flesh and made His dwelling among us. We have seen His glory, the glory of the One and Only, who came from the Father, full of grace and truth.

409   **1 Tim. 3:16** Beyond all question, the mystery of godliness is great: He appeared in a body.

410   **Col. 2:9** In Christ all the fullness of the Deity lives in bodily form.

411   **Is. 9:6** To us a child is born, to us a son is given, and the government will be on His shoulders. And He will be called Wonderful Counselor, Mighty God, Everlasting Father, Prince of Peace.

412   **Matt. 28:18** All authority in heaven and on earth has been given to Me.

413   **Matt. 28:20** Surely I am with you always, to the very end of the age.

414   **Acts 3:15** You killed the author of life.

415   **1 John 1:7** The blood of Jesus Christ, His Son, purifies us from every sin.

416   **Acts 20:28** Be shepherds of the church of God, which He bought with His own blood.

122. Why was it necessary for our Savior to be true man?

Christ had to be true man in order to

A. act in our place under the Law and fulfill it for us (active obedience);

417   **Gal. 4:4–5** When the time had fully come, God sent His Son, born of a woman, born under law, to redeem those under law, that we might receive the full rights of sons.

418   **Rom. 5:19** Just as through the disobedience of the one man the many were made sinners, so also through the obedience of the one man the many will be made righteous.

B. be able to suffer and die for our guilt because we failed to keep the Law (passive obedience).

419 **Col. 1:22** He has reconciled you by Christ's physical body through death to present you holy in His sight, without blemish and free from accusation.

420 **Heb. 2:14** Since the children have flesh and blood, He too shared in their humanity so that by His death He might destroy him who holds the power of death—that is, the devil.

123. Why was it necessary for our Savior to be true God?

Christ had to be true God in order that

A. His fulfilling of the Law, His life, suffering, and death might be a sufficient ransom for all people;

421 **Ps. 49:7** No man can redeem the life of another or give to God a ransom for him.

422 **Mark 10:45** The Son of Man did not come to be served, but to serve, and to give His life as a ransom for many.

423 **Rom. 3:22–24** There is no difference, for all have sinned, and fall short of the glory of God, and are justified freely by His grace through the redemption that came by Christ Jesus.

424 **Gal. 3:13** Christ redeemed us from the curse of the law by becoming a curse for us.

425 **Gal. 4:4–5** When the time had fully come, God sent His Son, born of a woman, born under law, to redeem those under law, that we might receive the full rights of sons.

426 **1 Peter 1:18–19** You know that it was not with perishable things such as silver or gold that you were

redeemed from the empty way of life handed down to you from your forefathers, but with the precious blood of Christ, a lamb without blemish or defect.

B. He might be able to overcome death and the devil for us.

427   **1 Cor. 15:57** Thanks be to God! He gives us the victory through our Lord Jesus Christ.

428   **2 Tim. 1:10** Our Savior, Christ Jesus . . . has destroyed death.

429   **Heb. 2:14** Since the children have flesh and blood, He too shared in their humanity so that by His death He might destroy him who holds the power of death—that is, the devil.

124. What do you therefore confess about Jesus Christ, the God-man?

I believe that Jesus Christ is my Lord and my Redeemer, whom I love and serve with my whole life.

430   **1 Cor. 6:20** You were bought at a price. Therefore honor God with your body.

Bible narrative: Thomas' confession **(John 20:24).**

The Office of Christ

125. For what threefold office was Christ anointed?

Christ was anointed to be our Prophet, Priest, and King.

A. As Prophet, Christ

1. preached personally during His life on earth, validating His word with miracles, especially His own resurrection;

431   **Deut. 18:15** The Lord your God will raise up for you a prophet like me from among your own brothers. You must listen to Him.

432   **Matt. 17:5** "This is My Son, whom I love; with Him I am well pleased. Listen to Him!"

433   **Mark 1:38** Let us go somewhere else—to the nearby villages—so I can preach there also. That is why I have come.

434   **John 1:17–18** The law was given through Moses; grace and truth came through Jesus Christ. No one has ever seen God, but God the One and Only, who is at the Father's side, has made Him known.

435   **John 6:68** Simon Peter answered Him, "Lord, to whom shall we go? You have the words of eternal life."

2. through the preached Gospel today still proclaims Himself to be the Son of God and Redeemer of the world.

436   **Mark 16:15** He said to them, "Go into all the world and preach the good news to all creation."

437   **Luke 10:16** He who listens to you listens to Me; he who rejects you rejects Me; but he who rejects Me rejects Him who sent Me.

438   **2 Cor. 5:20** We are therefore Christ's ambassadors, as though God were making His appeal through us. We implore you on Christ's behalf. Be reconciled to God.

B. As Priest, Christ

1. fulfilled the Law perfectly in our stead (active obedience);

439   **Gal. 4:4–5** When the time had fully come, God sent His Son, born of a woman, born under law, to

redeem those under law, that we might receive the full rights of sons.

2. sacrificed Himself for our sins (passive obedience);

440   **1 Cor. 15:3** Christ died for our sins according to the Scriptures.

441   **Heb. 7:26–27** Such a high priest meets our need—one who is holy, blameless, pure, set apart from sinners, exalted above the heavens. Unlike the other high priests, He does not need to offer sacrifices day after day, first for His own sins, and then for the sins of the people. He sacrificed for their sins once for all when He offered Himself.

442   **1 John 2:2** He is the atoning sacrifice for our sins, and not only for ours but also for the sins of the whole world.

3. still pleads for us with His heavenly Father (intercession).

443   **1 John 2:1** We have one who speaks to the Father in our defense—Jesus Christ, the Righteous One.

C. As King, Christ

1. rules with His almighty power over all creation (the kingdom of power—all creatures);

444   **Matt. 28:18** All authority in heaven and on earth has been given to Me.

2. governs and protects especially His church (the kingdom of grace—the church on earth);

445   **John 18:36–37** Jesus said, "My kingdom is not of this world. If it were, My servants would fight to prevent My arrest by the Jews. But now My kingdom is from another place." "You are a king, then!" said Pilate—Jesus answered, "You are right in saying I am

a king. In fact, for this reason I was born, and for this I came into the world, to testify to the truth. Everyone on the side of truth listens to Me."

3. finally leads His church to glory in heaven (the kingdom of glory—the church in heaven).

446   **2 Tim. 4:18** The Lord will rescue me from every evil attack and will bring me safely to His heavenly kingdom. To Him be glory for ever and ever. Amen.

The Savior in the State of Humiliation

126. What two states do the Scriptures distinguish in Christ's work of salvation?

A. The state of humiliation

B. The state of exaltation

127. What was Christ's humiliation?

Christ's humiliation was that as man He did not always or fully use His divine powers.

447   **Phil. 2:5–8** Let this mind be in you which was also in Christ Jesus, who, being in the form of God, did not consider it robbery to be equal with God, but made Himself of no reputation, taking the form of a servant, and coming in the likeness of men. And being found in appearance as a man, He humbled Himself and became obedient to the point of death, even the death of the cross (NKJV).

Bible narratives: Wedding at Cana **(John 2:1–11).** Raising of Lazarus **(John 11:38–44).** Rays of hidden glory **(John 18:1–6).**

128. Which words of the Apostles' Creed describe the stages of Christ's humiliation?

"Conceived by the Holy Spirit, born of the Virgin Mary, suffered under Pontius Pilate, was crucified, died and was buried."

129. What do the Scriptures teach about Christ's conception?

They teach that Christ, the Son of God, received a true human body and soul in the Virgin Mary through the miraculous power of the Holy Spirit, not through a human father.

448   **Luke 1:35** The Holy Spirit will come upon you, and the power of the Most High will overshadow you. So the holy one to be born will be called the Son of God.

449   **Matt. 1:20** Joseph son of David, do not be afraid to take Mary home as your wife, because what is conceived in her is from the Holy Spirit.

130. What do the Scriptures teach of the birth of Christ?

They teach that Jesus Christ, the God-man, was born of the Virgin Mary.

450   **Is. 7:14** The virgin will be with child and will give birth to a son, and will call Him Immanuel. (See also **Matt. 1:23**.)

451   **Luke 2:7** She gave birth to her firstborn, a son. She wrapped Him in cloths and placed Him in a manger, because there was no room for them in the inn.

Bible narrative: The virgin birth **(Matt. 1:18–25).**

131. What do the Scriptures teach about Christ's life, suffering, and death?

They teach that Christ

A. endured poverty, contempt, and persecution in His earthly life;

452   **2 Cor. 8:9** Though He was rich, yet for your sakes He became poor, so that you through His poverty might become rich.

453   **Matt. 8:20** Foxes have holes and birds of the air have nests, but the Son of Man has no place to lay His head.

454   **Is. 53:3** He was despised and rejected by men, a man of sorrows, and familiar with suffering. Like one from whom men hide their faces He was despised, and we esteemed Him not.

455   **John 8:40** You are determined to kill Me, a man who has told you the truth that I heard from God.

Bible narratives: At His birth Jesus had only strips of cloth and a manger **(Luke 2:7).** Herod tried to murder Him, but He escaped to Egypt **(Matt. 2:13).** In Nazareth the people tried to throw Him down from the brow of the hill **(Luke 4:29).** In the temple they picked up stones to stone Him **(John 8:59).**

B. suffered great agony of body and soul under Pontius Pilate;

456   **John 19:1–3** Pilate took Jesus and had Him flogged. The soldiers twisted together a crown of thorns and put it on His head. They clothed Him in a purple robe and went up to Him again and again, saying, "Hail, king of the Jews!" And they struck Him in the face.

Bible narrative: The suffering of Christ **(Mark 15:1–20).**

C. died in excruciating agony on the cross.

457   **John 19:16–18** Finally Pilate handed Him over to them to be crucified. So the soldiers took charge of Jesus. Carrying His own cross, He went out to the place of the Skull (which in Aramaic is called Golgotha). Here they crucified Him.

458   **Matt. 27:46** About the ninth hour Jesus cried out in a loud voice . . . "My God, My God, why have You forsaken Me?" (He suffered the tortures of the damned in hell.)

459   **John 19:30** He bowed His head and gave up His spirit.

Bible narrative: The death of Christ **(Mark 15:21–41).**

132. What do the Scriptures teach about Christ's burial?

They teach that Christ's body was buried in the tomb and remained there until the third day, without decaying in any way.

460   **Acts 13:37** The one whom God raised from the dead did not see decay.

Bible narrative: The burial of Christ **(Mark 15:42–47).**

Christ's Work of Redemption, or Atonement

133. Why did Christ humble Himself?

Christ voluntarily humbled Himself in order to "redeem me, a lost and condemned person."

461   **Is. 53:4–5** Surely He took up our infirmities and carried our sorrows, yet we considered Him stricken by God, smitten by Him, and afflicted. But He was pierced for our transgressions, He was crushed for our iniquities; the punishment that brought us peace was upon Him, and by His wounds we are healed.

462   **John 10:17–18** I lay down My life—only to take it up again. No one takes it from Me, but I lay it down of My own accord.

134. From what has Christ redeemed you?

He has redeemed me "from all sins, from death, and from the power of the devil."

463   **John 1:29** Look, the Lamb of God, who takes away the sin of the world!

464   **Heb. 2:14–15, 17** Since the children have flesh and blood, He too shared in their humanity so that by His death He might destroy him who holds the power of death—that is, the devil—and free those who all their lives were held in slavery by their fear of death. . . . For this reason He had to be made like His brothers in every way, in order that He might become a merciful and faithful high priest in service to God, and that He might make atonement for the sins of the people.

135. How has Christ redeemed you from all sins?

A. He took my guilt and punishment upon Himself.

465   **Rom. 5:19** Through the obedience of the one man the many will be made righteous.

466   **2 Cor. 5:21** God made Him who had no sin to be sin for us, so that in Him we might become the righteousness of God.

467   **Gal. 3:13** Christ redeemed us from the curse of the law by becoming a curse for us, for it is written: "Cursed is everyone who is hung on a tree."

B. He freed me from the slavery of sin.

468   **John 8:34, 36** I tell you the truth, everyone who sins is a slave to sin. . . . So if the Son sets you free, you will be free indeed.

469   **1 Peter 2:24** He Himself bore our sins in His body on the tree, so that we might die to sins and live for righteousness; by His wounds you have been healed.

136. How has Christ rescued you from death?

Through His suffering, death, and resurrection, Christ has triumphed over death. Since He now gives me eternal life I need not fear death.

470   **1 Cor. 15:55–57** "Where, O death, is your victory? Where, O death, is your sting?" The sting of death is sin, and the power of sin is the law. But thanks be to God! He gives us the victory through our Lord Jesus Christ.

471   **2 Tim. 1:10** Our Savior, Christ Jesus . . . has destroyed death and has brought life and immortality to light through the gospel.

472   **1 Peter 1:3** In His great mercy He has given us new birth into a living hope through the resurrection of Jesus Christ from the dead.

137. How has Christ rescued you from the power of the devil?

Christ has completely conquered the devil. Therefore the devil can no longer accuse me of my sins, and I can resist his temptations.

473   **Gen. 3:15** I will put enmity between you and the woman, and between your offspring and hers; He will crush your head, and you will strike His heel.

474   **1 John 3:8** The reason the Son of God appeared was to destroy the devil's work.

475   **James 4:7** Resist the devil, and he will flee from you.

Note: See also **Rom. 8:31–34; Col. 2:15; Heb. 2:14–15; 1 Peter 5:8–9; Rev. 12:10.**

138. With what has Christ redeemed you?

Christ has redeemed me, "not with gold or silver, but with His holy, precious blood and with His innocent suffering and death."

476   **Is. 53:5** By His wounds we are healed.

477   **1 Peter 1:18–19** You know that it was not with perishable things such as silver or gold that you were redeemed from the empty way of life handed down to you from your forefathers, but with the precious blood of Christ, a lamb without blemish or defect.

478   **1 John 1:7** The blood of Jesus, His Son, purifies us from all sin.

139. How does this work of redemption benefit you?

Christ was my substitute. He took my place under God's judgment against sin. By paying the penalty of my guilt, Christ atoned, or made satisfaction, for my sins (vicarious atonement).

479   **Is. 53:4–5** Surely He took up our infirmities and
       carried our sorrows, yet we considered Him stricken
       by God, smitten by Him, and afflicted. But He was
       pierced for our transgressions, He was crushed for
       our iniquities; the punishment that brought us peace
       was upon Him, and by His wounds we are healed.

480   **2 Cor. 5:21** God made Him who had no sin to be
       sin for us, so that in Him we might become the righ-
       teousness of God.

481   **Heb. 2:17** For this reason He had to be made like
       His brothers in every way, in order that He might
       become a merciful and faithful high priest in service
       to God, and that He might make atonement for the
       sins of the people.

140. Has Christ redeemed only you?

No, Christ has redeemed me and all people (universal atonement).

482   **2 Cor. 5:15** He died for all.

483   **2 Cor. 5:19** God was reconciling the world to
       Himself in Christ, not counting men's sins against
       them.

484   **1 Tim. 1:15** Here is a trustworthy saying that
       deserves full acceptance: Christ Jesus came into the
       world to save sinners—of whom I am the worst.

485   **1 John 2:2** He is the atoning sacrifice for our sins,
       and not only for ours but also for the sins of the
       whole world.

486   **2 Peter 2:1** [They deny the] Lord who bought
       them—bringing swift destruction on themselves.

The Savior in the State of Exaltation

141. What is Christ's exaltation?

Christ's exaltation is that as man He now fully and always uses His divine powers.

487   **Phil. 2:9–11** God exalted Him to the highest place and gave Him the name that is above every name, that at the name of Jesus every knee should bow, in heaven and on earth and under the earth, and every tongue confess that Jesus Christ is Lord, to the glory of God the Father.

142. Which words of the Apostles' Creed describe the stages of Christ's exaltation?

"He descended into hell. The third day He rose again from the dead. He ascended into heaven and sits at the right hand of God, the Father Almighty. From thence He will come to judge the living and the dead."

143. Why is Christ's descent into hell part of His exaltation?

The Scriptures teach that Christ, after He was made alive in His grave, descended into hell, not to suffer punishment, but to proclaim His victory over His enemies in hell.

488   **1 Peter 3:18–19** [Christ] was put to death in the body but made alive by the Spirit, through whom also He went and preached to the spirits in prison.

489   **Col. 2:15** Having disarmed the powers and authorities, He made a public spectacle of them, triumphing over them by the cross.

144. What do the Scriptures teach about Christ's resurrection?

They teach that on the third day Christ victoriously rose from the grave and showed Himself alive to His disciples.

490   **Acts 10:40–41** God raised Him from the dead on the third day and caused Him to be seen. He was not seen by all the people, but by witnesses whom God had already chosen—by us who ate and drank with Him after He rose from the dead.

491   **1 Cor. 15:4–8** He was raised on the third day according to the Scriptures, and . . . He appeared to Peter, and then to the Twelve. After that, He appeared to more than five hundred of the brothers at the same time, most of whom are still living, though some have fallen asleep. Then He appeared to James, then to all the apostles, and last of all He appeared to me also, as to one abnormally born.

492   **Acts 1:3** After His suffering, He showed Himself to these men and gave many convincing proofs that He was alive. He appeared to them over a period of forty days and spoke about the kingdom of God.

Bible narrative: Christ's resurrection **(Matt. 27:62–28:20; Mark 16; Luke 24; John 20–21).**

145. Why is Christ's resurrection so important and comforting?

Christ's resurrection proves that

A. Christ is the Son of God;

493   **Rom. 1:4** [He was] declared with power to be the Son of God by His resurrection from the dead.

B. His doctrine is the truth;

494 **John 2:19** Destroy this temple, and I will raise it again in three days.

495 **John 8:28** When you have lifted up the Son of Man, then you will know that I am the one I claim to be and that I do nothing on My own but speak just what the Father has taught Me.

C. God the Father accepted Christ's sacrifice for the reconciliation of the world;

496 **Rom. 4:25** [Christ] was delivered over to death for our sins and was raised to life for our justification.

497 **Rom. 5:10** If, when we were God's enemies, we were reconciled to Him through the death of His Son, how much more, having been reconciled, shall we be saved through His life!

498 **1 Cor. 15:17** If Christ has not been raised, your faith is futile; you are still in your sins.

D. all believers in Christ will rise to eternal life

499 **John 11:25–26** I am the resurrection and the life. He who believes in Me will live, even though he dies; and whoever lives and believes in Me will never die.

500 **John 14:19** Because I live, you also will live.

501 **1 Cor. 15:20** Christ has indeed been raised from the dead, the firstfruits of those who have fallen asleep.

146. What do the Scriptures teach about Christ's ascension?

They teach that 40 days after His resurrection, Christ, in the presence of His disciples, ascended bodily into the glory of His Father, to prepare a place for us in heaven.

502 **Luke 24:51** While He was blessing them, He left them and was taken up into heaven.

503   **Eph. 4:10** He who descended is the very one who ascended higher than all the heavens.

504   **John 14:2–3** In My Father's house are many rooms; if it were not so, I would have told you. I am going there to prepare a place for you. And if I go and prepare a place for you, I will come back and take you to be with Me that you also may be where I am.

505   **John 17:24** Father, I want those You have given Me to be with Me where I am, and to see My glory.

Bible narrative: Christ's ascension **(Acts 1:9–11).**

147. What does it mean that Christ sits at the right hand of God the Father Almighty?

With this expression Scripture teaches that Christ, as true man, is not only present everywhere, but also now fully exercises His divine power over the whole universe.

506   **Eph. 1:20–23** [God] seated Him [Christ] at His right hand in the heavenly realms, far above all rule and authority, power and dominion, and every title that can be given, not only in the present age but also in the one to come. And God placed all things under His feet and appointed Him to be head over everything for the church, which is His body, the fullness of Him who fills everything in every way.

148. What comfort do we get from Christ's ascension to the right hand of God?

We know that the exalted God-man, Christ

A. as our Prophet sends people to proclaim the saving Gospel by the power of the Holy Spirit;

507   **Eph. 4:10–12** [He] ascended higher than all the heavens, in order to fill the whole universe. It was He who gave some to be apostles, some to be

prophets, some to be evangelists, and some to be pastors and teachers, to prepare God's people for works of service, so that the body of Christ may be built up.

508   **Luke 10:16** He who listens to you listens to Me.

509   **John 16:7** It is for your good that I [Jesus] am going away. Unless I go away, the Counselor will not come to you; but if I go, I will send Him to you.

B. as our Priest pleads and prays for us before the Father;

510   **Rom. 8:34** [Christ] is at the right hand of God and is also interceding for us.

511   **1 John 2:1** If anybody does sin, we have one who speaks to the Father in our defense—Jesus Christ, the Righteous One.

C. as our King rules and protects His church and governs over all the world especially for the benefit of His church.

512   **Ps. 110:1** The Lord says to my Lord: "Sit at My right hand until I make Your enemies a footstool for Your feet."

Note: See **Eph. 1:20–23.**

149. What do the Scriptures teach about Christ's second coming?

A. Christ will return visibly and with great glory on the Last Day.

513   **Matt. 24:27** As lightning that comes from the east is visible even in the west, so will be the coming of the Son of Man.

514   **Luke 21:27** At that time they will see the Son of Man coming in a cloud with power and great glory.

515   **Acts 1:11** "Men of Galilee," they said, "why do you
        stand here looking into the sky? This same Jesus,
        who has been taken from you into heaven, will come
        back in the same way you have seen Him go into
        heaven."

516   **2 Peter 3:10** The day of the Lord will come like a
        thief. The heavens will disappear with a roar; the
        elements will be destroyed by fire, and the earth and
        everything in it will be laid bare.

517   **Rev. 1:7** Look, He is coming with the clouds, and
        every eye will see Him, even those who pierced Him;
        and all the peoples of the earth will mourn because
        of Him. So shall it be! Amen.

   B. Christ will return to judge the world, not to set up
an earthly government.

518   **Matt. 25:31–32** When the Son of Man comes in
        His glory, and all the angels with Him, He will sit on
        His throne in heavenly glory. All the nations will be
        gathered before Him, and He will separate the
        people one from another as a shepherd separates the
        sheep from the goats.

519   **John 12:48** There is a judge for the one who rejects
        Me and does not accept My words; that very word
        which I spoke will condemn him at the last day.

520   **John 18:36** Jesus said, "My kingdom is not of this
        world."

521   **2 Cor. 5:10** We must all appear before the judgment
        seat of Christ, that each one may receive what is due
        him for the things done while in the body, whether
        good or bad.

   Bible narrative: The final judgment **(Matt. 25:31–
46).**

Note: Millennialists teach the unscriptural doctrine that either before or after the return of Christ the church will experience a literal period of 1,000 years (a millennium) of peace and prosperity. **Revelation 20** speaks in picture language of Christ's spiritual rule on the earth through the Gospel and does not refer to earthly government.

C. Christ will return on a specific day known by God alone.

522   **Matt. 24:44** You also must be ready, because the Son of Man will come at an hour when you do not expect Him.

523   **Mark 13:32** No one knows about that day or hour, not even the angels in heaven, nor the Son, but only the Father.

524   **Acts 17:31** He has set a day when He will judge the world with justice by the man He has appointed.

Bible narrative: The parable of the 10 virgins **(Matt. 25:1–13).**

D. Before Christ returns, there will be increasing turmoil and distress for the church and the world.

525   **Matt. 24:7** Nation will rise against nation, and kingdom against kingdom. There will be famines and earthquakes in various places.

526   **Matt. 24:22** If those days had not been cut short, no one would survive, but for the sake of the elect those days will be shortened.

527   **1 Tim. 4:1** The Spirit clearly says that in later times some will abandon the faith and follow deceiving spirits and things taught by demons.

Bible narrative: Signs preceding Christ's coming **(Matthew 24).**

E. The return of Christ is a source of hope and joy for the Christian.

528   **Luke 21:28** When these things begin to take place, stand up and lift up your heads, because your redemption is drawing near.

529   **Heb. 9:28** Christ was sacrificed once to take away the sins of many people; and He will appear a second time, not to bear sin, but to bring salvation to those who are waiting for Him.

530   **Titus 2:13** We wait for the blessed hope—the glorious appearing of our great God and Savior, Jesus Christ.

531   **Rev. 22:20** He who testifies to these things says, "Yes, I am coming soon." Amen. Come, Lord Jesus.

Bible narrative: Encouraging words **(1 Thess. 4:13–18).**

150. In conclusion, then, why has Christ redeemed you?

The Scriptures teach that Christ's purpose was

A. "that I may be His own"; that is, I am now righteous and blameless in the sight of God;

532   **2 Cor. 5:21** God made Him who had no sins to be sin for us, so that in Him we might become the righteousness of God.

533   **Rev. 5:9** You were slain, and with Your blood You purchased men for God from every tribe and language and people and nation.

B. that I may "live under Him in His kingdom"; that is, that I am now freed from the slavery of sin and thus freed to serve God;

534   **Rom. 6:6** Our old man was crucified with Him, that the body of sin might be done away with, that we should no longer be slaves of sin (NKJV).

535   **2 Cor. 5:15** He died for all, that those who live should no longer live for themselves but for Him who died for them and was raised again.

536   **Col. 2:6** Just as you received Christ Jesus as Lord, continue to live in Him.

537   **Titus 2:14** [Jesus Christ] gave Himself for us to redeem us from all wickedness and to purify for Himself a people that are His very own, eager to do what is good.

C. that I may "serve Him in everlasting righteousness, innocence, and blessedness"; that is, that I honor God with my whole life and rejoice in Him now on earth and forever in heaven.

538   **Luke 1:69, 74–75** He has raised up a horn of salvation for us . . . to rescue us from the hand of our enemies, and to enable us to serve Him without fear in holiness and righteousness before Him all our days.

539   **Gal. 2:20** I have been crucified with Christ and I no longer live, but Christ lives in me. The life I live in the body, I live by faith in the Son of God, who loved me and gave Himself for me.

540   **1 Peter 2:9** You are a chosen people, a royal priesthood, a holy nation, a people belonging to God, that you may declare the praises of Him who called you out of darkness into His wonderful light.

Bible narrative: The saints in heaven **(Rev. 7:13–17).**

151. What is the basis of our faith and life in Christ?
"He is risen from the dead, lives and reigns to all eternity."

THE APOSTLES' CREED
147

541 **Col. 3:1–3** Since, then, you have been raised with Christ, set your hearts on things above, where Christ is seated at the right hand of God. Set your minds on things above, not on earthly things. For you died, and your life is now hidden with Christ in God.

152. Why do you close this article with the words, "This is most certainly true"?

Because all that I confess in this article is plainly taught in the Bible, and I, therefore, firmly believe it.

The Third Article

Sanctification

I believe in the Holy Spirit, the holy Christian church, the communion of saints, the forgiveness of sins, the resurrection of the body, and the life everlasting. Amen.

What does this mean? I believe that I cannot by my own reason or strength believe in Jesus Christ, my Lord, or come to Him; but the Holy Spirit has called me by the Gospel, enlightened me with His gifts, sanctified and kept me in the true faith.

In the same way He calls, gathers, enlightens, and sanctifies the whole Christian church on earth, and keeps it with Jesus Christ in the one true faith.

In this Christian church He daily and richly forgives all my sins and the sins of all believers.

On the Last Day He will raise me and all the dead, and give eternal life to me and all believers in Christ.

This is most certainly true.

153. What five points does this article discuss?

   I. *The Holy Spirit*
  II. *The Church, the Communion of Saints*
 III. *The Forgiveness of Sins*
 IV. *The Resurrection of the Body*
  V. *The Life Everlasting*

I. The Holy Spirit

The Person of the Holy Spirit

154. Who is the Holy Spirit?

The Holy Spirit is the third person in the Holy Trinity, true God with the Father and the Son—therefore not merely the power or energy of God.

542   **Matt. 28:19** Go and make disciples of all nations, baptizing them in the name of the Father and of the Son and of the Holy Spirit.

155. How do you know that the Holy Spirit is God?

Because the Scriptures clearly call Him God, teaching that

   A. the Holy Spirit has divine names;

543   **Acts 5:3–4** Peter said, "Ananias, how is it that Satan has so filled your heart that you have lied to the Holy Spirit? . . . You have not lied to men but to God."

544   **1 Cor. 3:16** Don't you know that you yourselves are God's temple and that God's Spirit lives in you?

   B. the Holy Spirit possesses divine attributes (properties or characteristics);

545   **Ps. 139:7–10** Where can I go from Your Spirit? Where can I flee from Your presence? If I go to the

heavens, You are there; if I make my bed in the depths, You are there. If I rise on the wings of the dawn, if I settle on the far side of the sea, even there Your hand will guide me, Your right hand will hold me fast. (Omnipresence)

546   **1 Cor. 2:10** The Spirit searches all things, even the deep things of God. (Omniscience)

547   **Heb. 9:14** Christ, who through the eternal Spirit offered Himself unblemished to God, cleanse our consciences from acts that lead to death, so that we may serve the living God! (Eternity)

Note: See **Matt. 28:19.** (Holiness)

C. the Holy Spirit does divine works (which only God can do);

548   **Gen. 1:2** Now the earth was formless and empty, darkness was over the surface of the deep, and the Spirit of God was hovering over the waters. (Creation)

549   **Titus 3:5** He saved us through the washing of rebirth and renewal by the Holy Spirit. (Sanctification)

D. the Holy Spirit receives divine honor and glory.

550   **1 Peter 4:14** The Spirit of glory and of God rests on you.

The Work of the Holy Spirit

156. What is the special work of the Holy Spirit?

The Holy Spirit sanctifies me (makes me holy) by bringing me to faith in Christ, so that I might have the blessings of redemption and lead a godly life (sanctification in the wide sense).

Note: The word *sanctification* is used in two ways:

1. The wide sense—the whole work of the Holy Spirit by which He brings us to faith and also enables us to lead a godly life.

2. The narrow sense—that part of the Holy Spirit's work by which He directs and empowers the believer to lead a godly life.

551   **1 Cor. 6:11** You were washed, you were sanctified, you were justified in the name of the Lord Jesus Christ and by the Spirit of our God.

157. Why do you need the Holy Spirit to begin and sustain this faith in you?

By nature I am spiritually blind, dead, and an enemy of God, as the Scriptures teach; therefore, "I cannot by my own reason or strength believe in Jesus Christ, my Lord, or come to Him."

552   **1 Cor. 2:14** The man without the Spirit does not accept the things that come from the Spirit of God, for they are foolishness to him, and he cannot understand them, because they are spiritually discerned.

553   **Eph. 2:1** You were dead in your transgressions and sins.

554   **Rom. 8:7** The sinful mind is hostile to God.

555   **Eph. 2:8–9** By grace you have been saved, through faith—and this not from yourselves, it is the gift of God—not by works, so that no one can boast.

556   **1 Cor. 12:3** No one can say, "Jesus is Lord," except by the Holy Spirit.

158. What has the Holy Spirit done to bring you to faith?

The Holy Spirit "has called me by the Gospel," that

is, He has invited and drawn me by the Gospel to partake of the spiritual blessings that are mine in Christ.

557   **Rom. 1:16** I am not ashamed of the gospel, because it is the power of God for the salvation of everyone who believes: first for the Jew, then for the Gentile.

558   **2 Thess. 2:14** He called you to this through our gospel.

559   **Rev. 22:17** The Spirit and the bride say, "Come!" And let him who hears say, "Come!" Whoever is thirsty, let him come; and whoever wishes, let him take the free gift of the water of life.

Bible narratives: Invitation to the wedding banquet of the king's son **(Matt. 22:1–10).** Invitation to the great banquet **(Luke 14:16–17).**

159. How do the Scriptures describe this gracious work of the Spirit in you?

The Scriptures teach that by the Gospel the Holy Spirit "enlightened me with His gifts," that is, He gave me the saving knowledge of Jesus, my Savior, so that I trust, rejoice, and find comfort in Him.

560   **1 Peter 2:9** You are a chosen people, a royal priesthood, a holy nation, a people belonging to God, that you may declare the praises of Him who called you out of darkness into His wonderful light.

561   **2 Cor. 4:6** God, who said, "Let light shine out of darkness," made His light shine in our hearts to give us the light of the knowledge of the glory of God in the face of Christ.

562   **1 Peter 1:8** Even though you do not see Him now, you believe in Him and are filled with an inexpressible and glorious joy.

563   **Rom. 15:13** The God of hope fill you with all joy
        and peace as you trust in Him, so that you may over-
        flow with hope by the power of the Holy Spirit.

Bible narratives: The Samaritans were filled with great
joy when Philip preached Christ to them **(Acts 8:5–8)**.
The jailer at Philippi and his whole family were filled
with joy because they had come to believe **(Acts 16:
25–34)**.

160. What is this work of the Holy Spirit called?

It is called conversion (being turned) or regeneration
(new birth).

564   **Ps. 51:13** I will teach transgressors Your ways, and
        sinners will turn back to You. (Conversion)
565   **John 3:5–6** Jesus answered, "I tell you the truth, no
        one can enter the kingdom of God unless he is born
        of water and the Spirit. Flesh gives birth to flesh, but
        the Spirit gives birth to spirit." (Regeneration)

161. Why do you say that the Holy Spirit has done this by the Gospel?

The Gospel is the means by which the Holy Spirit
offers us all the blessings of Christ and creates faith in
us.

Note: The written and spoken Word of the Gospel
and the sacraments are the means of grace.

566   **John 17:20** My prayer is not for them alone. I pray
        also for those who will believe in Me through their
        message.
567   **Rom. 10:17** Faith comes from hearing the message,
        and the message is heard through the word of
        Christ.

568   **1 Cor. 4:15** In Christ Jesus I became your father through the Gospel.

569   **1 Peter 1:23** You have been born again, not of perishable seed, but of imperishable, through the living and enduring word of God.

570   **Titus 3:5** He saved us through the washing of rebirth and renewal by the Holy Spirit. (Baptism)

571   **John 20:22–23** With that He breathed on them and said, "Receive the Holy Spirit. If you forgive anyone his sins, they are forgiven; if you do not forgive them, they are not forgiven." (Absolution)

572   **Matt. 26:27–28** He took the cup, gave thanks and offered it to them, saying, "Drink from it, all of you. This is My blood of the covenant [testament], which is poured out for many for the forgiveness of sins." (Lord's Supper)

162. Besides faith, what else does the Holy Spirit create in you by the Gospel?

The Holy Spirit sanctifies me in the true faith, that is, by faith He works a renewal of my whole life—in spirit, will, attitude, and desires—so that I now strive to overcome sin and do good works (sanctification in the narrow sense).

573   **Ps. 51:10** Create in me a pure heart, O God, and renew a steadfast spirit within me.

574   **Rom. 8:9** You, however, are controlled not by the sinful nature but by the Spirit, if the Spirit of God lives in you. And if anyone does not have the Spirit of Christ, he does not belong to Christ.

575   **2 Cor. 5:17** If anyone is in Christ, he is a new creation.

576   **Gal. 5:22–23** The fruit of the Spirit is love, joy,
         peace, patience, kindness, goodness, faithfulness,
         gentleness and self-control.

577   **Eph. 2:10** For we are God's workmanship, created
         in Christ Jesus to do good works, which God
         prepared in advance for us to do.

578   **Eph. 5:18–20** Do not get drunk on wine, which
         leads to debauchery. Instead, be filled with the
         Spirit. Speak to one another with psalms, hymns and
         spiritual songs. Sing and make music in your heart
         to the Lord, always giving thanks to God the Father
         for everything, in the name of our Lord Jesus Christ.

163. What are good works in God's sight?

In God's sight a good work is everything that a child
of God does, speaks, or thinks in faith according to the
Ten Commandments, for the glory of God, and for the
benefit of his or her neighbor.

579   **Heb.11:6** Without faith it is impossible to please
         God.

580   **John 15:5** If a man remains in Me and I in him, he
         will bear much fruit; apart from Me you can do
         nothing.

581   **Matt. 15:9** They worship Me in vain; their teachings
         are but rules taught by men.

582   **John 14:15** If you love Me, you will obey what
         command.

583   **1 Cor. 10:31** Whether you eat or drink or whatever
         you do, do it all for the glory of God.

584   **Gal. 5:13** Serve one another in love.

Bible narratives: The widow's offering **(Mark 12:41–
44).** The expensive perfume poured on Jesus' head
(Mark 14:3–9). Mary and Martha **(Luke 10:38–42).**

164. What do the Scriptures teach about the gifts of the Holy Spirit?

The Scriptures teach that the Holy Spirit gives gifts to His church. They teach that

A. the Holy Spirit through the Word and sacraments freely gives to all Christians the most precious gifts: faith in Christ, the forgiveness of sins, and eternal life;

B. in apostolic times the Holy Spirit also gave some Christians the gift to perform miraculous signs and wonders (for example, healings, speaking in tongues, raising the dead).

The Scriptures do not teach, however, that God will necessarily give all Christians in every time and place special miraculous gifts. The Holy Spirit bestows His blessings according to His good pleasure.

585 **2 Cor. 12:12** The things that mark an apostle—signs, wonders and miracles—were done among you with great perseverance.

586 **Eph. 2:20–22** [You are] built on the foundation of the apostles and prophets, with Christ Jesus Himself as the chief cornerstone. In Him the whole building is joined together and rises to become a holy temple in the Lord. And in Him you too are being built together to become a dwelling in which God lives by His Spirit.

Bible narrative: Special signs connected with the apostles personally **(Acts 5:12–16; 8:14–19; 19:11–12, 20; 20:7–12).**

Note: In popular English, the word *charismatic* describes a dynamic person, highly emotional worship, or claims of special miraculous gifts. But the Greek word *charisma* means simply "gift" and refers, for example, to Christ's whole work of salvation **(Rom. 5:15–16),** to eternal life **(Rom. 6:23),** and to being married or single **(1 Cor. 7:7).**

165. Finally, what also does the Holy Spirit do for you?

The Holy Spirit by the Gospel keeps me in the true faith.

587   **Phil. 1:6** He who began a good work in you will carry it on to completion until the day of Christ Jesus.

588   **1 Peter 1:5** [You] through faith are shielded by God's power until the coming of the salvation.

589   **1 Thess. 2:13** The word of God . . . is at work in you who believe.

166. Whom else does the Holy Spirit regenerate and renew?

The Holy Spirit "calls, gathers, enlightens, and sanctifies the whole Christian church on earth, and keeps it with Jesus Christ in the one true faith."

590   **Eph. 3:6** Through the gospel the Gentiles are heirs together with Israel, members together of one body, and sharers together in the promise in Christ Jesus.

167. Does the Holy Spirit want to do this in the lives of all people?

God the Holy Spirit earnestly wants to convert all people and bring them to salvation through the Gospel.

591   **Ezek. 33:11** I take no pleasure in the death of the wicked, but rather that they turn from their ways and live.

592   **1 Tim. 2:4** [God] wants all men to be saved and to come to a knowledge of the truth.

593   **2 Peter 3:9** The Lord . . . is patient with you, not
        wanting anyone to perish, but everyone to come to
        repentance.

168. Then, why are not all people saved?

Many reject the Word and resist the Holy Spirit;
therefore they remain in unbelief and under God's judgment by their own fault.

594   **Matt. 23:37** O Jerusalem, Jerusalem, you who kill
        the prophets and stone those sent to you, how often
        I have longed to gather your children together, as a
        hen gathers her chicks under her wings, but you
        were not willing.

595   **Acts 7:51** You stiff-necked people, with uncircum-
        cised hearts and ears! You are just like your fathers:
        You always resist the Holy Spirit!

Bible narratives: The invited guests refused to come
(Matt. 22:1–10). The guests refused to accept the invitation **(Luke 14:16–24).**

II. The Church, the Communion of Saints

169. What is the holy Christian church?

The holy Christian church is the communion of
saints, the total number of those who believe in Christ.
All believers in Christ, but only believers, are members
of the church (invisible church).

596   **Eph. 2:19–22** You are no longer foreigners and
        aliens, but fellow citizens with God's people and
        members of God's household, built on the founda-
        tion of the apostles and prophets, with Christ Jesus
        Himself as the chief cornerstone. In Him the whole

building is joined together and rises to become a holy temple in the Lord. And in Him you too are being built together to become a dwelling in which God lives by His Spirit.

597   **John 10:16** I have other sheep that are not of this sheep pen. I must bring them also. They too will listen to My voice, and there shall be one flock and one shepherd.

598   **Rom. 8:9** If anyone does not have the Spirit of Christ, he does not belong to Christ.

170. Why do you say, "I believe" in the church?

A. Because faith, which makes people members of the church, is invisible, the church is invisible to human eyes.

599   **Luke 17:20–21** The kingdom of God does not come with your careful observation, nor will people say, "Here it is," or "There it is," because the kingdom of God is within you.

600   **2 Tim. 2:19** God's solid foundation stands firm, sealed with this inscription: "The Lord knows those who are His."

B. The Scriptures assure us that the Holy Spirit continues to gather and preserve the church.

601   **Matt. 16:18** You are Peter, and on this rock I will build My church, and the gates of Hades will not overcome it.

602   **Acts 2:41, 47** Those who accepted his message were baptized, and about three thousand were added to their number that day. . . . And the Lord added to their number daily those who were being saved.

Bible narrative: The seven thousand in Israel (**1 Kings 19:8–18**).

171. Why do you say, I believe in "the" church?

There is only one church, one spiritual body of believers (saints), whose one and only head is Christ.

603   **Rom. 12:4–5** As each of us has one body with many members . . . so in Christ we who are many form one body.

604   **Eph. 4:3–6** Make every effort to keep the unity of the Spirit through the bond of peace. There is one body and one Spirit—just as you were called to one hope when you were called—one Lord, one faith, one baptism; one God and Father of all, who is over all and through all and in all.

605   **Col. 1:18** [Christ] is the head of the body, the church.

172. Why is the church called "holy"?

It is made up of holy people (saints), believers who have been cleansed by the blood of Christ and who serve God with holy living.

606   **Eph. 5:25–27** Christ loved the church and gave Himself up for her to make her holy, cleansing her by the washing with water through the word, and to present her to Himself as a radiant church, without stain or wrinkle or any other blemish, but holy and blameless.

607   **1 Peter 2:5** You also, like living stones, are being built into a spiritual house to be a holy priesthood, offering spiritual sacrifices acceptable to God through Jesus Christ.

173. Why is the church called "Christian"?

It belongs to Christ and is built on Him alone.

608   **1 Cor. 3:11** No one can lay any foundation other than the one already laid, which is Jesus Christ.

609 **Eph. 2:20** [You are] built on the foundation of the apostles and prophets, with Christ Jesus Himself as the chief cornerstone.

Note: The word *catholic,* sometimes used in creeds, means "universal" or "general." The church exists throughout the world, wherever the Gospel is proclaimed.

174. Where is the holy Christian church to be found?

The holy Christian church is to be found where "the Gospel is preached in its purity and the holy sacraments are administered according to the Gospel" (Augsburg Confession VII 1). The Gospel and the sacraments are called the "marks of the church."

610 **Is. 55:10–11** As the rain and the snow come down from heaven, and do not return to it without watering the earth and making it bud and flourish, so that it yields seed for the sower and bread for the eater, so is My word that goes out from My mouth: It will not return to Me empty, but will accomplish what I desire and achieve the purpose for which I sent it.

175. In what other senses is the word church used?

The word *church* is also used to indicate
A. the visible church of God;
B. a denomination;
C. a local congregation;
D. a house of worship.

176. Why does Scripture call local congregations "church"?

Local, visible gatherings around the means of grace are called churches because there believers are gathered around Word and sacrament.

611   **Matt. 18:17** If he refuses to listen to them, tell it to the church; and if he refuses to listen even to the church, treat him as you would a pagan or a tax collector.

612   **Matt. 28:19–20** Go and make disciples of all nations, baptizing them in the name of the Father and of the Son and of the Holy Spirit, and teaching them to obey everything I have commanded you. And surely I am with you always, to the very end of the age.

613   **1 Cor. 1:2** To the church of God in Corinth, to those sanctified in Christ Jesus and called to be holy, together with all those everywhere who call on the name of our Lord Jesus Christ—their Lord and ours.

Note: Paul wrote to the churches in Galatia **(Gal. 1:2)**. He wrote to the church of the Thessalonians **(1 Thess. 1:1).** John wrote to the seven churches of Asia Minor **(Revelation 1–3).** A group of congregations is also called "church" **(Acts 9:31).**

177. What is the visible church?

The visible church is the whole number of those who use the Word of God and profess the Christian faith, but among whom, beside the true Christians, there are also unbelievers.

178. Are there then two churches, one visible and the other invisible?

There is only one church—all believers in Christ. The visible gathering is called church because of the believers gathered around the means of grace in an assembly in which there are also hypocrites.

Bible narratives: The net that caught all kinds of fish **(Matt. 13:47–48)**. A man without wedding clothes **(Matt. 22:11–12)**. Ananias and Sapphira **(Acts 5: 1–11)**.

179. What do the Scriptures teach about our life in the church?

They teach that

A. we should seek always to be and remain members of the invisible church, Christ's body, by sincere faith in Christ, our Savior;

614   **John 15:5** I am the vine; you are the branches. If a man remains in Me and I in him, he will bear much fruit; apart from Me you can do nothing.

615   **2 Cor. 13:5** Examine yourselves to see whether you are in the faith; test yourselves.

B. we should be faithful to that visible church, or denomination, which professes and teaches all of the Bible's doctrine purely and administers the sacraments according to Christ's institution;

616   **John 8:31–32** If you hold to My teaching, you are really My disciples. Then you will know the truth, and the truth will set you free.

617   **Acts 2:42** They devoted themselves to the apostles' teaching and to the fellowship, to the breaking of bread and to prayer.

618   **1 Cor. 1:10** I appeal to you, brothers, in the name
        of our Lord Jesus Christ, that all of you agree with
        one another so that there may be no divisions
        among you and that you may be perfectly united in
        mind and thought.

Note: A religious denomination is a church body or
organization with a distinct name and a distinct body of
doctrine.

C. we should avoid false teachers, false churches, and
all organizations that promote a religion that is contrary
to God's Word;

619   **Matt. 7:15–16** Watch out for false prophets. They
        come to you in sheep's clothing, but inwardly they
        are ferocious wolves. By their fruit you will recognize
        them.

620   **Rom. 16:17–18** I urge you, brothers, to watch out
        for those who cause divisions and put obstacles in
        your way that are contrary to the teaching you have
        learned. Keep away from them. For such people are
        not serving our Lord Christ, but their own appetites.
        By smooth talk and flattery they deceive the minds
        of naive people.

621   **2 Cor. 6:14** Do not be yoked together with unbe-
        lievers. (See also **vv. 15–18.**)

622   **Gal. 1:8** Even if we or an angel from heaven should
        preach a gospel other than the one we preached to
        you, let him be eternally condemned!

623   **2 Tim. 4:3** The time will come when men will not
        put up with sound doctrine. Instead, to suit their
        own desires, they will gather around them a great
        number of teachers to say what their itching ears
        want to hear.

624   **1 John 4:1** Dear friends, do not believe every spirit, but test the spirits to see whether they are from God, because many false prophets have gone out into the world.

D. we should maintain and extend God's church by telling others about Jesus Christ, by personal service, and by prayer and financial support.

625   **John 20:21** As the Father has sent Me, I am sending you.

626   **Acts 1:8** You will receive power when the Holy Spirit comes on you; and you will be My witnesses in Jerusalem, and in all Judea and Samaria, and to the ends of the earth.

627   **Acts 8:1, 4** On that day a great persecution broke out against the church at Jerusalem, and all except the apostles were scattered throughout Judea and Samaria. . . . Those who had been scattered preached the word wherever they went.

628   **1 Peter 2:9** You are a chosen people, a royal priesthood, a holy nation, a people belonging to God, that you may declare the praises of Him who called you out of darkness into His wonderful light.

629   **1 Peter 3:15** Always be prepared to give an answer to everyone who asks you to give the reason for the hope that you have. But do this with gentleness and respect.

630   **Luke 10:2** He told them, "The harvest is plentiful, but the workers are few. Ask the Lord of the harvest, therefore, to send out workers into His harvest field."

631   **Gal. 6:6** Anyone who receives instruction in the word must share all good things with his instructor.

Bible narratives: Peter addressed the crowds **(Acts**

2:17–39; 3:12–26). Philip witnessed to the eunuch **(Acts 8:26–35).** The early Christians prayed for the spreading of the Gospel **(Acts 4:23–30).** They also contributed to the support of the ministry **(Phil. 4:16–19).**

III. The Forgiveness of Sins

180. Why do you say, "I believe in the forgiveness of sins"?

I believe in the forgiveness of sins because through Christ God has declared pardon and forgiveness to all sinful humanity.

632   **Ps. 130:3–4** If you, O Lord, kept a record of sins, O Lord, who could stand? But with You there is forgiveness; therefore You are feared.

633   **2 Cor. 5:19** God was reconciling the world to Himself in Christ, not counting men's sins against them.

181. What moves God to forgive sins?

God forgives sins because He is merciful and because of Christ's atoning sacrifice for sinners.

634   **Ps. 86:15** You, O Lord, are a compassionate and gracious God, slow to anger, abounding in love and faithfulness.

635   **John 3:16** God so loved the world that He gave His one and only Son, that whoever believes in Him shall not perish but have eternal life.

636   **Eph. 1:7** In [Christ] we have redemption through His blood, the forgiveness of sins, in accordance with the riches of God's grace.

637   **1 John 2:2** He is the atoning sacrifice for our sins, and not only for ours but also for the sins of the whole world.

182. How is it possible for a just and holy God to declare sinners righteous (justification)?

God declares sinners righteous for Christ's sake; that is, our sins have been imputed or charged to Christ, the Savior, and Christ's righteousness has been imputed or credited to us.

638   **2 Cor. 5:21** God made Him who had no sin to be sin for us, so that in Him we might become the righteousness of God.

639   **Rom. 3:22–24** There is no difference, for all have sinned and fall short of the glory of God, and are justified freely by His grace through the redemption that came by Christ Jesus.

640   **Rom. 4:25** He was delivered over to death for our sins and was raised to life for our justification.

Bible narrative: The king forgave the servant all his debts **(Matt. 18:23–35).**

183. Where does God offer the forgiveness of sins?

God offers the forgiveness of sins in the Gospel.

641   **Luke 24:47** Repentance and forgiveness of sins will be preached in His name to all nations.

642   **Rom. 1:16** I am not ashamed of the gospel, because it is the power of God for the salvation of everyone who believes: first for the Jew, then for the Gentile.

643   **2 Cor. 5:19** He has committed to us the message of reconciliation.

184. How do you receive this forgiveness of sins?

I receive this forgiveness through faith, that is, by believing the Gospel.

644 **Gen. 15:6** Abram believed the Lord, and He credited it to him as righteousness.

645 **Rom. 3:28** A man is justified by faith apart from observing the law.

646 **Rom. 4:5** To the man who does not work but trusts God who justifies the wicked, his faith is credited as righteousness.

Bible narrative: The tax collector in the temple **(Luke 18:9–14)**.

185. Why can and should I be sure of the forgiveness of my sins?

I can and should be sure of the forgiveness of my sins because God keeps His promises in Christ.

647 **Rom. 8:38–39** I am convinced that neither death nor life, neither angels nor demons, neither the present nor the future, nor any powers, neither height nor depth, nor anything else in all creation, will be able to separate us from the love of God that is in Christ Jesus our Lord.

648 **2 Tim. 1:12** I know whom I have believed, and am convinced that He is able to guard what I have entrusted to Him for that day.

186. Why must we firmly hold to this teaching of justification by grace, for Christ's sake, through faith?

We must firmly hold to this teaching because

A. it is the most important doctrine of the Christian religion;

649   **Acts 4:12** Salvation is found in no one else, for there is no other name under heaven given to men by which we must be saved.

650   **Acts 10:43** All the prophets testify about Him that everyone who believes in Him receives forgiveness of sins through His name.

B. it distinguishes the Christian religion from false religions, all of which teach salvation by works;

651   **Gal. 5:4–5** You who are trying to be justified by law have been alienated from Christ; you have fallen away from grace. But by faith we eagerly await through the Spirit the righteousness for which we hope.

Note: See **Micah 7:18–20.**

C. it gives enduring comfort to the penitent sinner;

652   **Acts 16:30–31, 34** "Sirs, what must I do to be saved?" They replied, "Believe in the Lord Jesus, and you will be saved—you and your household.". . . He was filled with joy, because he had come to believe in God.

653   **Matt. 9:2** Take heart, son; your sins are forgiven.

D. it gives all glory to God for His grace and mercy in Christ.

654   **Rev. 1:5–6** To Him who loves us and has freed us from our sins by His blood, and has made us to be a kingdom and priests to serve His God and Father—to Him be glory and power for ever and ever! Amen.

IV. The Resurrection of the Body

187. *What do the Scriptures teach about the resurrection of the body?*

They teach that on the Last Day Christ "will raise me and all the dead." The same bodies that have died shall be made alive.

655   **Job 19:25–27** I know that my Redeemer lives, and that in the end He will stand upon the earth. And after my skin has been destroyed, yet in my flesh I will see God; I myself will see Him with my own eyes—I, and not another.

656   **John 5:28–29** A time is coming when all who are in their graves will hear His voice and come out.

657   **1 Thess. 4:16** The Lord Himself will come down from heaven, with a loud command, with the voice of the archangel and with the trumpet call of God, and the dead in Christ will rise first.

188. *Are people reborn in bodies or forms?*

Reincarnation, the belief that when people die they are reborn in other bodies or in a series of other bodies, is contrary to Scripture.

658   **Heb. 9:27–28** Just as man is destined to die once, and after that to face judgment, so Christ was sacrificed once to take away the sins of many people; and He will appear a second time, not to bear sin, but to bring salvation to those who are waiting for Him.

Note: See **1 Corinthians 15.**

189. What difference will there be between believers and unbelievers in the resurrection?

A. The believers will rise with glorified bodies and enter everlasting life in heaven with God.

659   **Dan. 12:2** Multitudes who sleep in the dust of the earth will awake: some to everlasting life, others to shame and everlasting contempt.

660   **John 5:28–29** All who are in their graves will hear His voice and come out—those who have done good will rise to live, and those who have done evil will rise to be condemned.

661   **1 Cor. 15:42–43** So will it be with the resurrection of the dead. The body that is sown is perishable, it is raised imperishable; it is sown in dishonor, it is raised in glory; it is sown in weakness, it is raised in power.

662   **Phil. 3:21** [Christ] will transform our lowly bodies so that they will be like His glorious body.

B. The unbelievers will rise to eternal death, that is, to shame and torment in hell forever.

663   **Is. 66:24** Their worm will not die, nor will their fire be quenched, and they will be loathsome to all mankind.

664   **Matt. 10:28** Do not be afraid of those who kill the body but cannot kill the soul. Rather, be afraid of the One who can destroy both soul and body in hell.

665   **Matt. 25:41** He will say to those on His left, "Depart from Me, you who are cursed, into the eternal fire prepared for the devil and his angels."

666   **Rev. 1:7** Look, He is coming with the clouds, and every eye will see Him, even those who pierced Him; and all the peoples of the earth will mourn because of Him. So shall it be! Amen.

Bible narrative: The story of the rich man and Lazarus illustrates that there are only two places **(Luke 16:19–31)**.

V. The Life Everlasting

190. To whom does God give eternal life?

God gives eternal life to me and all believers in Christ.

A. Eternal life is a present possession.

667   **John 17:3** This is eternal life: that they may know You, the only true God, and Jesus Christ, whom You have sent.

668   **John 3:16** God so loved the world that He gave His one and only Son, that whoever believes in Him shall not perish but have eternal life.

669   **Rom. 10:9** If you confess with your mouth, "Jesus is Lord," and believe in your heart that God raised Him from the dead, you will be saved.

670   **John 3:36** Whoever believes in the Son has eternal life, but whoever rejects the Son will not see life, for God's wrath remains on him.

B. At the time of death, the soul of a believer is immediately with Christ in heaven.

671   **Eccl. 12:7** The dust returns to the ground it came from, and the spirit returns to God who gave it.

672   **Luke 23:43** I tell you the truth, today you will be with Me in paradise.

673   **John 17:24** Father, I want those You have given Me to be with Me where I am, and to see My glory, the glory You have given Me because You loved Me before the creation of the world.

674   **Phil. 1:23–24** I desire to depart and to be with
       Christ, which is better by far; but it is more neces-
       sary for you that I remain in the body.

675   **Rev. 14:13** I heard a voice from heaven say, "Write:
       Blessed are the dead who die in the Lord from now
       on." "Yes," says the Spirit, "they will rest from their
       labor, for their deeds will follow them."

C. At the Last Day the believers, in both body and
soul, will begin the full enjoyment of being with Christ
forever.

676   **1 Cor. 15:51–52** Listen, I tell you a mystery: We
       will not all sleep, but we will all be changed—in a
       flash, in the twinkling of an eye, at the last trumpet.
       For the trumpet will sound, the dead will be raised
       imperishable, and we will be changed.

677   **Matt. 25:34** Then the King [Jesus] will say to those
       on His right, "Come, you who are blessed by My
       Father; take your inheritance, the kingdom prepared
       for you since the creation of the world."

678   **Ps. 16:11** You will fill me with joy in Your presence,
       with eternal pleasures at Your right hand.

679   **Rom. 8:18** I consider that our present sufferings are
       not worth comparing with the glory that will be
       revealed in us.

680   **1 John 3:2** Dear friends, now we are children of
       God, and what we will be has not yet been made
       known. But we know that when He appears, we
       shall be like Him, for we shall see Him as He is.

191. Are you sure that you have eternal life?

Even as I now believe in Christ my Savior, I also know
that I have been chosen to eternal life out of pure grace
in Christ without any merit of my own and that no one

can pluck me out of His hand (eternal election of grace or predestination).

681   **John 10:27–28** My sheep listen to My voice; I know them, and they follow Me. I give them eternal life, and they shall never perish; no one can snatch them out of My hand.

682   **Rom. 8:28–30** We know that in all things God works for the good of those who love Him, who have been called according to His purpose. For those God foreknew He also predestined to be conformed to the likeness of His Son, that He might be the first-born among many brothers. And those He predestined, He also called; those He called, He also justified; those He justified, He also glorified.

683   **Eph. 1:3–6** Praise be to the God and Father of our Lord Jesus Christ, who has blessed us in the heavenly realms with every spiritual blessing in Christ. For He chose us in Him before the creation of the world to be holy and blameless in His sight. In love He predestined us to be adopted as His sons through Jesus Christ, in accordance with His pleasure and will—to the praise of His glorious grace, which He has freely given us in the One He loves.

192. Why do you close this article with the words "This is most certainly true"?

Because all that I confess in this article is plainly taught in the Bible and therefore I firmly believe it.

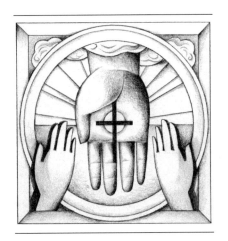

THE LORD'S PRAYER

193. What privilege and command does God give to those who believe in Jesus Christ?

God commands and invites believers in Jesus Christ to pray.

684   **Matt. 7:7–8** Ask and it will be given to you; seek and you will find; knock and the door will be opened to you. For everyone who asks receives; he who seeks finds; and to him who knocks, the door will be opened.

685   **1 Thess. 5:16–18** Be joyful always; pray continually; give thanks in all circumstances, for this is God's will for you in Christ Jesus.

194. What is prayer?

Prayer is speaking to God in words and thoughts.

686   **Ps. 19:14** May the words of my mouth and the
       meditation of my heart be pleasing in Your sight,
       O Lord, my Rock and my Redeemer.
687   **Acts 7:59–60** While they were stoning him, Stephen
       prayed, "Lord Jesus, receive my spirit." Then he fell on
       his knees and cried out, "Lord, do not hold this sin
       against them." When he had said this, he fell asleep.

Bible narratives: Abraham prayed for Sodom **(Gen.
18:22–23).** Jesus in Gethsemane **(Matt. 26:36–44).**
Thanksgiving for the release of Peter and John from
prison **(Acts 4:23–31).**

195. To whom should we pray?

We should pray to the true God only, Father, Son,
and Holy Spirit, not to idols, saints, or anything God
has created.

688   **Ps. 65:2** O You who hear prayer, to You all men will
       come.
689   **1 John 5:20–21** We are in Him who is true—even
       in His Son Jesus Christ. He is the true God and
       eternal life. Dear children, keep yourselves from
       idols.
690   **Rev. 22:8–9** I, John, am the one who heard and saw
       these things. And when I had heard and seen them,
       I fell down to worship at the feet of the angel who
       had been showing them to me. But he said to me,
       "Do not do it! I am a fellow servant with you and
       with your brothers the prophets and of all who keep
       the words of this book. Worship God!"

Bible narratives: Elijah and the priests of Baal **(1 Kings
18:25–29, 36–39).** Daniel in the lions' den **(Dan. 6:
1–23).** Paul in Lystra **(Acts 14:8–18).** Jesus' High
Priestly Prayer **(John 17).**

196. Whose prayers are acceptable to God?

Only those who believe in Jesus Christ may pray to God and expect to be heard.

691   **John 14:13–14** I will do whatever you ask in My name, so that the Son may bring glory to the Father. You may ask Me for anything in My name, and I will do it.

692   **John 15:7** If you remain in Me and My words remain in you, ask whatever you wish, and it will be given you.

197. What should be the content of our prayers.

In our prayers we should ask for everything that tends to the glory of God and to our own and our neighbor's welfare, both spiritual and bodily blessings. We should also praise and thank God for who He is and what He has done.

693   **Phil. 4:6** Do not be anxious about anything, but in everything, by prayer and petition, with thanksgiving, present your requests to God.

694   **Ps. 136:1** Give thanks to the Lord, for He is good. His love endures forever.

198. How should we pray?

We should pray

A. in the name of Jesus, that is, with faith in Him as our Redeemer;

695   **John 16:23** I tell you the truth, My Father will give you whatever you ask in My name.

B. with confidence, that is with firm trust that for Jesus' sake our prayers will be answered;

696   **Matt. 21:22** If you believe, you will receive whatever you ask for in prayer.

697   **James 1:6–7** When he asks, he must believe and not doubt, because he who doubts is like a wave of the sea, blown and tossed by the wind. That man should not think he will receive anything from the Lord.

C. according to God's revealed will.

698   **Luke 11:13** If you then, though you are evil, know how to give good gifts to your children, how much more will your Father in heaven give the Holy Spirit to those who ask Him!

699   **Luke 22:42** Father, if You are willing, take this cup from Me; yet not My will, but Yours be done.

700   **Matt. 8:2** A man with leprosy came and knelt before Him and said, "Lord, if You are willing, You can make me clean."

701   **1 John 5:14** This is the confidence we have in approaching God: that if we ask anything according to His will, He hears us.

199. Who helps us pray?

God the Holy Spirit prays with and for us.

702   **Rom. 8:26** In the same way, the Spirit helps us in our weakness. We do not know what we ought to pray for, but the Spirit Himself intercedes for us with groans that words cannot express.

200. How does God answer prayer?

God hears the prayers of all Christians and answers in His own way and at His own time.

703   **Is. 65:24** Before they call I will answer; while they are still speaking I will hear.

704   **2 Cor. 12:8–9** Three times I pleaded with the Lord to take it away from me. But He said to me, "My grace is sufficient for you, for My power is made

perfect in weakness." Therefore I will boast all the more gladly about my weaknesses, so that Christ's power may rest on me.

Bible narratives: Jesus healed a centurion's servant **(Matt. 8:5–13).** Jesus healed a paralytic **(Matt. 9:1–8).** The Lord planned to rescue Israel from Egypt **(Ex. 3:7–10).** The parable of the persistent widow **(Luke 18:1–8).**

201. For whom should we pray?

We should pray for ourselves and for all other people, even for our enemies, but not for the souls of the dead.

705   **1 Tim. 2:1–2** I urge, then, first of all, that requests, prayers, intercession and thanksgiving be made for everyone—for kings and all those in authority, that we may live peaceful and quiet lives in all godliness and holiness.

706   **Matt. 5:44** Pray for those who persecute you.

707   **Heb. 9:27** Man is destined to die once, and after that to face judgment.

Bible narratives: The tax collector prayed for himself **(Luke 18:13).** Abraham prayed for Sodom **(Gen. 18:23–32).** The Canaanite woman prayed for her daughter **(Matt. 15:22–28).** Jesus prayed for His enemies **(Luke 23:34).** Stephen prayed for his enemies **(Acts 7:60).**

202. Where should we pray?

We should pray everywhere, especially when we are alone, with our families, and in church.

708   **1 Tim. 2:8** I want men everywhere to lift up holy hands in prayer, without anger or disputing.

709   **Matt. 6:6** When you pray, go into your room, close the door and pray to your Father, who is unseen. Then your Father, who sees what is done in secret, will reward you.

710   **Luke 5:16** Jesus often withdrew to lonely places and prayed.

711   **Acts 12:5** Peter was kept in prison, but the church was earnestly praying to God for him.

203. When should we pray?

We should pray regularly and frequently, especially in time of trouble.

712   **Ps. 65:8** Where morning dawns and evening fades You call forth songs of joy.

713   **Ps. 119:164** Seven times a day I praise You for Your righteous laws.

714   **Dan. 6:10** When Daniel learned that the decree had been published, he went home to his upstairs room where the windows opened toward Jerusalem. Three times a day he got down on his knees and prayed, giving thanks to his God, just as he had done before.

715   **Luke 18:1** Jesus told his disciples a parable to show them that they should always pray and not give up.

716   **1 Thess. 5:17–18** Pray continually; give thanks in all circumstances, for this is God's will for you in Christ Jesus.

717   **Ps. 50:15** Call upon Me in the day of trouble; I will deliver you, and you will honor Me.

Bible narrative: The early Christians kept the customary hours of prayer **(Acts 2:46–3:1; 10).**

Note: See Luther's suggestions in this catechism for daily morning, evening, and mealtime prayers.

204. What prayer did Jesus give us to show us how to pray?

Jesus gave us the Lord's Prayer.

Bible narrative: The Lord's Prayer **(Matt. 6:9–13; Luke 11:1–4).**

The Introduction

Our Father who art in heaven.

Our Father in heaven.

What does this mean? With these words God tenderly invites us to believe that He is our true Father and that we are His true children, so that with all boldness and confidence we may ask Him as dear children ask their dear father.

205. In what way does the word Father *in the Lord's Prayer encourage us to pray?*

The word *Father* tells us that God loves us and wants us to pray to Him confidently and without fear.

718   **1 John 3:1** How great is the love the Father has lavished on us, that we should be called children of God! And that is what we are! The reason the world does not know us is that it did not know Him.

719   **Rom. 8:15–16** You received the Spirit of sonship. . . . The Spirit Himself testifies with our spirit that we are God's children.

720   **2 Cor. 6:18** I will be a Father to you, and you will be My sons and daughters, says the Lord Almighty.

721   **Heb. 4:16** Let us then approach the throne of grace with confidence, so that we may receive mercy and find grace to help us in our time of need.

722   **Ps. 103:13** As a father has compassion on his chil-

dren, so the Lord has compassion on those who fear Him.

Bible narrative: The lost son **(Luke 15:11–32).**

206. What does the word our **impress upon us when we pray, "Our Father"?**

In Jesus all believers are children of the one Father and should pray with and for one another.

723 **Eph. 4:6** [There is] one God and Father of all, who is over all and through all and in all.

724 **Gal. 3:26** You are all sons of God through faith in Christ Jesus.

725 **James 5:16** Confess your sins to each other and pray for each other so that you may be healed. The prayer of a righteous man is powerful and effective.

207. What do the words who art [are] in heaven **say about God?**

These words assure us that our heavenly Father, as Lord over all, has the power to grant our prayers.

726 **Ps. 124:8** Our help is in the name of the Lord, the Maker of heaven and earth.

727 **Luke 1:37** Nothing is impossible with God.

728 **Acts 17:24** The God who made the world and everything in it is the Lord of heaven and earth.

The First Petition

Hallowed be Thy name.

Hallowed be Your name.

What does this mean? God's name is certainly holy in itself, but we pray in this petition that it may be kept holy among us also.

How is God's name kept holy? God's name is kept holy when the Word of God is taught in its truth and purity, and we, as the children of God, also lead holy lives according to it. Help us to do this, dear Father in heaven! But anyone who teaches or lives contrary to God's Word profanes the name of God among us. Protect us from this, heavenly Father!

208. *What is the connection between this petition and the Second Commandment?*

Both speak about the name of God. "In this petition we pray for exactly the same thing that God demands in the Second Commandment: that His name should not be taken in vain . . . but used rightly to the praise and glory of God" (Large Catechism III 45).

729   **Ex. 20:7** You shall not misuse the name of the Lord your God, for the Lord will not hold anyone guiltless who misuses His name.

209. *What are we asking when we pray that God's name be made holy?*

Since God's name is God as He has revealed Himself to us, we cannot make His name holy, but we do pray that He would help us keep His name holy in our lives.

730   **Ps. 103:1** Praise the Lord, O my soul; all my inmost being, praise His holy name.

210. *How do we keep God's name holy?*

We keep God's name holy

A. when God's Word is taught among us in its truth and purity;

731   **Jer. 23:28** Let the one who has My word speak it faithfully.

732   **John 17:17** Sanctify them by the truth; Your word is truth.

B. when we live according to the Word of God.

733   **Matt. 5:16** Let your light shine before men, that they may see your good deeds and praise your Father in heaven.

734   **Eph. 4:1** As a prisoner for the Lord, then, I urge you to live a life worthy of the calling you have received.

Bible narrative: Zacchaeus resolved to live the Christian life **(Luke 19:1–9).**

211. How is God's name profaned?

God's name is profaned, that is, dishonored,

A. when anyone teaches contrary to God's Word;

735   **Jer. 23:31** "Yes," declares the Lord, "I am against the prophets who wag their own tongues and yet declare, 'The Lord declares.' "

B. when anyone lives contrary to God's Word.

736   **Rom. 2:23–24** You who brag about the law, do you dishonor God by breaking the law? As it is written: "God's name is blasphemed among the Gentiles because of you."

The Second Petition

Thy kingdom come.

Your kingdom come.

What does this mean? The kingdom of God certainly comes by itself without our prayer, but we pray in this petition that it may come to us also.

How does God's kingdom come? God's kingdom comes when our heavenly Father gives us His Holy Spirit, so that by His grace we believe His holy Word and lead godly lives here in time and there in eternity.

212. What is the kingdom of God?

The kingdom of God is His ruling as king over the whole universe (kingdom of power), the church on earth (kingdom of grace), and the church and angels in heaven (kingdom of glory).

737   **Ps. 103:19** The Lord has established His throne in heaven, and His kingdom rules over all. (Kingdom of power)

738   **John 3:5** Jesus answered, I tell you the truth, no one can enter the kingdom of God unless he is born of water and the Spirit." (Kingdom of grace)

739   **2 Tim. 4:18** The Lord will rescue me from every evil attack and will bring me safely to His heavenly kingdom. To Him be glory for ever and ever. Amen. (Kingdom of glory)

213. For what do we pray in the Second Petition?

We do not pray that God's kingdom of power would come, because that is already present everywhere, but we ask God to

A. give us His Holy Spirit so that we believe His Word and lead godly lives as members of His kingdom of grace;

740   **Mark 1:15** "The time has come," He said. "The kingdom of God is near. Repent and believe the good news!"

741   **Rom. 14:17** The kingdom of God is not a matter of

eating and drinking, but of righteousness, peace and joy in the Holy Spirit.

742   **Col. 1:13–14** He has rescued us from the dominion of darkness and brought us into the kingdom of the Son He loves, in whom we have redemption, the forgiveness of sins.

  B. bring many others into His kingdom of grace;

743   **Matt. 9:38** Ask the Lord of the harvest, therefore, to send out workers into His harvest field.

744   **2 Thess. 3:1** Finally, brothers, pray for us that the message of the Lord may spread rapidly and be honored, just as it was with you.

  C. use us to extend His kingdom of grace;

745   **Acts 4:29** Now, Lord, consider their threats and enable Your servants to speak Your word with great boldness.

746   **1 Peter 2:12** Live such good lives among the pagans that, though they accuse you of doing wrong, they may see your good deeds and glorify God on the day He visits us.

  D. hasten the coming of His kingdom of glory.

747   **Phil. 3:20** Our citizenship is in heaven. And we eagerly await a Savior from there, the Lord Jesus Christ.

748   **Rev. 22:20** He who testifies to these things says, "Yes, I am coming soon." Amen. Come, Lord Jesus.

214. How can we be certain that the kingdom of God comes?

The Lord guarantees that His means of grace establish and sustain His kingdom.

749   **Is. 55:11** My word . . . will accomplish what I desire and achieve the purpose for which I sent it.

Bible narrative: The parable of the growing seed **(Mark 4:26–29).**

The Third Petition

Thy will be done on earth as it is in heaven.

Your will be done on earth as in heaven.

What does this mean? The good and gracious will of God is done even without our prayer, but we pray in this petition that it may be done among us also.

How is God's will done? God's will is done when He breaks and hinders every evil plan and purpose of the devil, the world, and our sinful nature, which do not want us to hallow God's name or let His kingdom come;

and when He strengthens and keeps us firm in His Word and faith until we die.

This is His good and gracious will.

215. What is the good and gracious will of God?

It is God's will that His name be kept holy and that His kingdom come, that is, that His Word be taught correctly and that sinners be brought to faith in Christ and lead godly lives.

750   **Deut. 4:2** Do not add to what I command you and do not subtract from it, but keep the commands of the Lord your God that I give you.

751   **John 6:40** My Father's will is that everyone who looks to the Son and believes in Him shall have eternal life, and I will raise him up at the last day.

752   **1 Tim. 2:4** [God] wants all men to be saved and to come to a knowledge of the truth.

753 **1 Thess. 4:3** It is God's will that you should be sanctified.

216. *Whose will and plans are opposed to the will of God?*

The devil, the world, and our own sinful nature oppose the good and gracious will of God.

754 **1 Peter 5:8** Be self-controlled and alert. Your enemy the devil prowls around like a roaring lion looking for someone to devour.

755 **1 John 2:15–17** Do not love the world or anything in the world. If anyone loves the world, the love of the Father is not in him. For everything in the world—the cravings of sinful man, the lust of his eyes and the boasting of what he has and does—comes not from the Father but from the world. The world and its desires pass away, but the man who does the will of God lives forever.

756 **Rom. 7:18** I know that nothing good lives in me, that is, in my sinful nature. For I have the desire to do what is good, but I cannot carry it out.

Bible narratives: The devil misled humanity to sin **(Gen 3:1–7).** The enemies of Jesus brought about the fall of Peter **(Luke 22:54–62).** Achan's sinful nature led him to steal **(Joshua 7:18–22).**

217. *Why do we pray that the will of God be done?*

We know that the will of God will always be done, but we want God's good and gracious will to be done in our lives.

"As God's name must be hallowed and His kingdom must come even without our prayer, so must His will be done and prevail even though the devil and all his host storm and rage furiously against it in their attempt utterly to exterminate the Gospel. But for our own sake we must pray that His will may be done among us without hindrance, in spite of their fury, so that they may accomplish nothing and we may remain steadfast" (Large Catechism III 68).

757 **Ps. 115:3** Our God is in heaven; He does whatever pleases Him.

758 **Ps. 43:3** Send forth Your light and Your truth, let them guide me; let them bring me to Your holy mountain, to the place where You dwell.

759 **Phil. 1:21** To me, to live is Christ and to die is gain.

Bible narrative: The helplessness of the enemies of God **(Psalm 2)**. The conversion of Paul **(Acts 9:1–19)**.

218. How is God's will done in our lives?

God's will is done when

A. He breaks and hinders the plans of the devil, the world, and our sinful nature, which try to destroy our faith in Christ Jesus;

760 **Rom. 16:20** The God of peace will soon crush Satan under your feet. The grace of our Lord Jesus be with you.

761 **2 Tim. 1:12** I know whom I have believed, and am convinced that He is able to guard what I have entrusted to Him for that day.

B. He strengthens and keeps us firm in His Word and faith and helps us lead God-pleasing lives;

762 **1 Peter 1:5** [You] through faith are shielded by God's power until the coming of the salvation that is ready to be revealed in the last time.

763   **Ps. 119:35** Direct me in the path of Your commands, for there I find delight.

C. He supports us in all our troubles until we die.

764   **Rom. 8:28** We know that in all things God works for the good of those who love Him, who have been called according to His purpose.

765   **2 Cor. 12:9** He said to me, "My grace is sufficient for you, for My power is made perfect in weakness."

Bible narratives: God hindered the evil will of Joseph's brothers and kept him faithful **(Gen. 50:15–21)**. God would not let the devil destroy Job **(Job 1:1–2:6).**

The Fourth Petition

Give us this day our daily bread.

Give us today our daily bread.

What does this mean? God certainly gives daily bread to everyone without our prayers, even to all evil people, but we pray in this petition that God would lead us to realize this and to receive our daily bread with thanksgiving.

What is meant by daily bread? Daily bread includes everything that has to do with the support and needs of the body, such as food, drink, clothing, shoes, house, home, land, animals, money, goods, a devout husband or wife, devout children, devout workers, devout and faithful rulers, good government, good weather, peace, health, self-control, good reputation, good friends, faithful neighbors, and the like.

219. Why do we pray to God for daily bread?

We pray to God for daily bread, which includes everything that has to do with the support and needs of the body, because Christ wants us to

A. realize that our entire life and that of everyone else depends on God;

766   **Ps. 145:15–16** The eyes of all look to You, and You give them their food at the proper time. You open Your hand and satisfy the desires of every living thing.

767   **Matt. 5:45** He causes His sun to rise on the evil and the good, and sends rain on the righteous and the unrighteous.

768   **Acts 17:28** In Him we live and move and have our being.

769   **James 4:15** You ought to say, "If it is the Lord's will, we will live and do this or that."

B. receive all our physical blessings with thanksgiving;

770   **Ps. 106:1** Give thanks to the Lord, for He is good; His love endures forever.

771   **Eph. 5:19–20** Sing and make music in your heart to the Lord, always giving thanks to God the Father for everything, in the name of our Lord Jesus Christ.

772   **1 Tim. 4:4–5** Everything God created is good, and nothing is to be rejected if it is received with thanksgiving, because it is consecrated by the word of God and prayer.

C. look to God for physical as well as spiritual blessings.

773   **Ps. 91:15** He will call upon Me, and I will answer

him; I will be with him in trouble, I will deliver him and honor him.

774 **Matt. 6:33** Seek first His kingdom and His righteousness, and all these things will be given to you as well.

775 **Luke 7:3** The centurion heard of Jesus and sent some elders of the Jews to Him, asking Him to come and heal his servant.

Bible narratives: Jesus healed blind Bartimaeus **(Mark 10:46–52).** Jesus healed 10 lepers **(Luke 17:11–19).**

220. How does God provide our daily bread?

He makes the earth fruitful and blesses us with the ability to work for the things we need.

776 **Ps. 104:14** He makes grass grow for the cattle, and plants for man to cultivate—bringing forth food from the earth.

777 **2 Thess. 3:10–12** Even when we were with you, we gave you this rule: "If a man will not work, he shall not eat." We hear that some among you are idle. They are not busy; they are busybodies. Such people we command and urge in the Lord Jesus Christ to settle down and earn the bread they eat.

221. What does God want us to do for those who are unable to work for daily food?

God does not want us to be selfish but to share with those who are unable to work and to include them in our prayers for daily bread.

778 **1 Tim. 5:8** If anyone does not provide for his relatives, and especially for his immediate family, he has denied the faith and is worse than an unbeliever.

779   **Heb. 13:16** Do not forget to do good and to share
        with others, for with such sacrifices God is pleased.
780   **1 John 3:17–18** If anyone has material possessions
        and sees his brother in need but has no pity on him,
        how can the love of God be in him? Dear children,
        let us not love with words or tongue but with actions
        and in truth.

*222. Why does Jesus have us say "this day" and
"daily"?*

These words teach us not to be greedy or wasteful or
to worry about the future but to live contentedly in the
confidence that the Lord will give us what we need.

781   **Prov. 30:8–9** Give me neither poverty nor riches,
        but give me only my daily bread. Otherwise, I may
        have too much and disown You and say, "Who is the
        Lord?" Or I may become poor and steal, and so
        dishonor the name of my God.
782   **Matt. 6:34** Do not worry about tomorrow, for
        tomorrow will worry about itself. Each day has
        enough trouble of its own.
783   **John 6:12** When they had all had enough to eat, He
        said to His disciples, "Gather the pieces that are left
        over. Let nothing be wasted."
784   **1 Tim. 6:8** If we have food and clothing, we will be
        content with that.
785   **1 Peter 5:7** Cast all your anxiety on Him because
        He cares for you.

Bible narrative: The parable of the rich fool (**Luke
12:15–21**).

The Fifth Petition

And forgive us our trespasses as we forgive those who trespass against us.

Forgive us our sins as we forgive those who sin against us.

What does this mean? We pray in this petition that our Father in heaven would not look at our sins, or deny our prayer because of them. We are neither worthy of the things for which we pray, nor have we deserved them, but we ask that He would give them all to us by grace, for we daily sin much and surely deserve nothing but punishment. So we too will sincerely forgive and gladly do good to those who sin against us.

223. What do we confess when we pray this petition?

We confess that we sin every day and deserve nothing but punishment.

786   **Prov. 28:13** He who conceals his sins does not prosper, but whoever confesses and renounces them finds mercy.

224. What do we ask for in this petition?

We ask that our Father in heaven would for Christ's sake graciously forgive our sins.

787   **Ps. 19:12** Who can discern his errors? Forgive my hidden faults.

788   **Ps. 51:1–2** Have mercy on me, O God, according to Your unfailing love; according to Your great compassion blot out my transgressions. Wash away all my iniquity and cleanse me from my sin.

789   **Ps. 130:3–4** If You, O Lord, kept a record of sins, O Lord, who could stand? But with You there is forgiveness; therefore You are feared.

790   **Luke 18:13** God, have mercy on me, a sinner.

225. Why do we include a prayer for forgiveness of sins in these petitions to our heavenly Father?

We are not worthy of the things for which we pray and have not deserved them. We therefore need God's forgiveness so that we may pray to Him confidently and in good conscience.

"Where the heart is not right with God . . . it will never dare to pray. . . . A confident and joyful heart can come only from the knowledge that our sins are forgiven" (Large Catechism III 92).

791   **Gen. 32:10** I am unworthy of all the kindness and faithfulness You have shown Your servant.

792   **Ps. 32:5** I said, "I will confess my transgressions to the Lord"—and You forgave the guilt of my sin.

226. What does God want us to do for those who sin against us?

Our heavenly Father wants us to forgive and to do good to those who sin against us.

793   **Matt. 6:12** Forgive us our debts, as we also have forgiven our debtors.

794   **Matt. 18:21–22** Peter came to Jesus and asked, "Lord, how many times shall I forgive my brother when he sins against me? Up to seven times?" Jesus answered, "I tell you, not seven times, but seventy-seven times."

795   **Eph. 4:32** Be kind and compassionate to one another, forgiving each other, just as in Christ God forgave you.

227. What does it show when we forgive others?

It shows that we truly believe that God has forgiven us.

"Inasmuch as we sin greatly against God every day and yet He forgives it all through grace, we must always forgive our neighbor who does us harm, violence, and injustice [and] bears malice toward us. . . . If you do not forgive, do not think that God forgives you" (Large Catechism III 94–95).

796 **Matt. 6:14–15** If you forgive men when they sin against you, your heavenly Father will also forgive you. But if you do not forgive men their sins, your Father will not forgive your sins.

Bible narratives: Joseph forgave his brothers **(Gen. 50:15–21).** The parable of the unmerciful servant **(Matt. 18:23–35).**

The Sixth Petition

And lead us not into temptation.

Lead us not into temptation.

What does this mean? God tempts no one. We pray in this petition that God would guard and keep us so that the devil, the world, and our sinful nature may not deceive us or mislead us into false belief, despair, and other great shame and vice. Although we are attacked by these things, we pray that we may finally overcome them and win the victory.

228. What do tempt and temptation mean in the Scriptures?

In the Scriptures these words have two meanings:

A. The testing of our faith, which God uses to bring us closer to Himself.

797   **John 6:5–6** When Jesus looked up and saw a great crowd coming toward Him, He said to Philip, "Where shall we buy bread for these people to eat?" He asked this only to test him, for He already had in mind what He was going to do.

798   **James 1:2–3** Consider it pure joy, my brothers, whenever you face trials of many kinds, because you know that the testing of your faith develops perseverance.

Bible narratives: The Lord tested Abraham by commanding him to sacrifice Isaac **(Gen. 22:1–19).** Jesus tested the faith of the Canaanite woman **(Matt. 15: 21–28).**

B. The attempts of our spiritual enemies to lure us away from God and His ways.

799   **Mark 14:38** Watch and pray so that you will not fall into temptation. The spirit is willing, but the body is weak.

800   **James 1:13–14** When tempted, no one should say, "God is tempting me." For God cannot be tempted by evil, nor does He tempt anyone; but each one is tempted when, by his own evil desire, he is dragged away and enticed.

229. Into what kinds of evil do our spiritual enemies try to mislead us?

The devil, the world, and our sinful nature try to mislead us into false belief, despair, and other great sins.

801   **1 Peter 5:8–9** Be self-controlled and alert. Your enemy the devil prowls around like a roaring lion looking for someone to devour. Resist him, standing

firm in the faith, because you know that your
brothers throughout the world are undergoing the
same kind of sufferings.

802   **Prov. 1:10** My son, if sinners entice you, do not give
in to them.

803   **Matt. 18:7** Woe to the world because of the things
that cause people to sin! Such things must come,
but woe to the man through whom they come!

804   **Gal. 5:17** The sinful nature desires what is contrary
to the Spirit, and the Spirit what is contrary to the
sinful nature.

805   **2 Cor. 4:8** We are hard pressed on every side, but
not crushed; perplexed, but not in despair.

Bible narratives: The devil tempted Eve to doubt and
disobey God **(Genesis 3).** The devil tempted Judas to
betray Christ **(John 13:2)** and to despair **(Matt. 27:
4–5).** Among enemies of Christ, Peter denied his Savior
(Luke 22:54–60). King David's sinful nature tempted
him to commit adultery and murder **(2 Sam. 12:9).**

230. What do we ask God to do for us when we pray this petition?

We ask our Father in heaven to give us strength to
resist and overcome temptations.

806   **Luke 22:31–32** Simon, Simon, Satan has asked to
sift you as wheat. But I have prayed for you, Simon,
that your faith may not fail.

807   **Rom. 13:14** Clothe yourselves with the Lord Jesus
Christ, and do not think about how to gratify the
desires of the sinful nature.

808   **1 Cor. 10:12–13** If you think you are standing firm,
be careful that you don't fall! No temptation has
seized you except what is common to man. And God

is faithful; He will not let you be tempted beyond what you can bear. But when you are tempted, He will also provide a way out so that you can stand up under it.

809 **Eph. 6:11, 17** Put on the full armor of God so that you can take your stand against the devil's schemes. . . . Take the helmet of salvation and the sword of the Spirit, which is the word of God.

Bible narratives: Joseph withstood the temptation of Potiphar's wife **(Gen. 39:1–20).** Jesus was tempted by Satan and won the victory for us **(Matt. 4:1–11).**

The Seventh Petition

But deliver us from evil.

But deliver us from evil.

What does this mean? We pray in this petition, in summary, that our Father in heaven would rescue us from every evil of body and soul, possessions and reputation, and finally, when our last hour comes, give us a blessed end, and graciously take us from this valley of sorrow to Himself in heaven.

231. What kind of prayer is the Seventh Petition?

The seventh petition is a summary petition in which we ask our Father in heaven to rescue us from the devil and all evil which has come into the world because of sin.

810 **Ps. 121:7–8** The Lord will keep you from all harm. He will watch over your life; the Lord will watch over your coming and going both now and forevermore.

811 **2 Thess. 3:3** The Lord is faithful, and He will strengthen and protect you from the evil one.

232. How does the Lord rescue us from every evil of body and soul, possessions and reputation?

In a world ruined by sin, the Lord keeps us from harm and helps us to endure the troubles that He allows to come into our lives.

812   **Acts 14:22** We must go through many hardships to enter the kingdom of God.

813   **Ps. 91:9–10** If you make the Most High your dwelling—even the Lord, who is my refuge—then no harm will befall you, no disaster will come near your tent.

814   **2 Cor. 12:9** My grace is sufficient for you, for My power is made perfect in weakness.

815   **Prov. 3:11–12** My son, do not despise the Lord's discipline and do not resent His rebuke, because the Lord disciplines those He loves, as a father the son he delights in.

Bible narratives: The three men in the fiery furnace **(Daniel 3).** Daniel in the lions' den **(Daniel 6).**

233. What final deliverance from evil do we ask the Lord to bring to us?

We want our Father in heaven to keep us faithful to Him and when we die to take us from this sorrowful world to Himself in heaven.

816   **Luke 2:29–30** Lord, as You have promised, You now dismiss Your servant in peace. For my eyes have seen Your salvation, which You have prepared in the sight of all people, a light for revelation to the Gentiles and for glory to Your people Israel.

817   **2 Tim. 4:18** The Lord will rescue me from every evil attack and will bring me safely to His heavenly kingdom. To Him be glory for ever and ever. Amen.

818   **Rev. 14:13** Blessed are the dead who die in the Lord.
819   **Rev. 21:4** He will wipe every tear from their eyes. There will be no more death or mourning or crying or pain, for the old order of things has passed away.

The Conclusion

For Thine is the kingdom and the power and the glory forever and ever. Amen.

For the kingdom, the power, and the glory are Yours now and forever. Amen.

What does this mean? This means that I should be certain that these petitions are pleasing to our Father in heaven, and are heard by Him; for He Himself has commanded us to pray in this way and has promised to hear us. Amen, amen, which means "yes, yes, it shall be so."

234. Why do we end the Lord's Prayer with the word amen?

The word *amen* means "so shall it be" and emphasizes that God, who has commanded us to pray, will hear our prayers and answer them as He has promised.

820   **Ps. 50:15** Call upon Me in the day of trouble; I will deliver you, and you will honor Me.
821   **Prov. 15:8** The Lord detests the sacrifice of the wicked, but the prayer of the upright pleases Him.
822   **Prov. 15:29** The Lord is far from the wicked but He hears the prayer of the righteous.

235. How do I know God is able to answer the prayers of His people in Christ Jesus?

A. He alone is the King who has all good gifts in His control.

823   **James 1:17** Every good and perfect gift is from above, coming down from the Father of the heavenly lights, who does not change like shifting shadows.

824   **Ps. 103:2–3** Praise the Lord, O my soul, and forget not all His benefits—who forgives all your sins and heals all your diseases.

B. He alone has the power to grant our petitions.

825   **Ps. 33:6** By the word of the Lord were the heavens made, their starry host by the breath of His mouth.

826   **Eph. 3:20–21** To Him who is able to do immeasurably more than all we ask or imagine, according to His power that is at work within us, to Him be glory in the church and in Christ Jesus throughout all generations, for ever and ever! Amen.

C. He has all glory and is worthy of our praise.

827   **Ps. 113:4–5** The Lord is exalted over all the nations, His glory above the heavens. Who is like the Lord our God, the One who sits enthroned on high?

828   **1 Tim. 1:17** To the King eternal, immortal, invisible, the only God, be honor and glory for ever and ever. Amen.

THE SACRAMENTS

236. What is a sacrament?

A sacrament is a sacred act

A. instituted by God,

B. in which God Himself has joined His Word of promise to a visible element,

C. and by which He offers, gives, and seals the forgiveness of sins earned by Christ.

Note: The word *sacrament* comes to us from the Latin Bible, where it translates the Greek word *mystery*. At first this word described all the saving truths of the faith, such as the Trinity, the incarnation, the redemption, the church (see for instance **1 Cor. 4:1; Eph. 5:32;** and **1 Tim. 3:16**). Later it was narrowed down to our present sense.

237. How many such sacraments are there?

By this definition there are two sacraments: Holy Baptism and the Lord's Supper.

Note: Sometimes Holy Absolution is counted as a third sacrament, even though it has no divinely instituted visible element (Large Catechism IV 74; Apology XIII 4).

829   **Acts 2:38** Peter replied, "Repent and be baptized, every one of you, in the name of Jesus Christ for the forgiveness of your sins. And you will receive the gift of the Holy Spirit."

830   **1 Cor. 10:16** The cup of blessing which we bless, is it not the communion of the blood of Christ? The bread which we break, is it not the communion of the body of Christ? (NKJV).

238. Why are we to treasure the sacraments, when water, bread, and wine are such common elements?

"The sacraments and all the external things ordained and instituted by God should be regarded not according to the gross, external mask (as we see the shell of a nut) but as that in which God's Word is enclosed" (Large Catechism IV 19).

831   **1 Cor. 1:28** God chose the lowly things of this world and the despised things—and the things that are not—to nullify the things that are.

Bible narrative: By God's promise the plain Jordan River had the power to cure Naaman's leprosy **(2 Kings 5:1–14).**

THE SACRAMENT OF HOLY BAPTISM

I. The Nature of Baptism

First

What is Baptism?

Baptism is not just plain water, but it is the water included in God's command and combined with God's word.

Which is that word of God?

Christ our Lord says in the last chapter of Matthew: "Therefore go and make disciples of all nations, baptizing them in the name of the Father and of the Son and of the Holy Spirit." **[Matt. 28:19]**

239. What does the word baptize mean?

Baptize means to apply water by immersing, washing, pouring, and the like.

832 **Mark 7:4** When they [the Pharisees] come from the marketplace they do not eat unless they wash. And they observe many other traditions, such as the washing [baptizing] of cups, pitchers, and kettles.

Note: To baptize with the Holy Spirit **(Matt. 3:11)** means to "pour out" the Spirit **(Acts 1:5** and **Acts 2:17–18)**.

240. What is so special about the water of Baptism?

"It is nothing else than a divine water, not that the water in itself is nobler than other water but that God's Word and commandment are added to it" (Large Catechism IV 14).

241. Who instituted Holy Baptism?

God Himself instituted Baptism, for our Lord Jesus Christ commanded His church to baptize all nations.

833 **Matt. 28:19–20** Go and make disciples of all nations, baptizing them in the name of the Father and of the Son and of the Holy Spirit, and teaching them to obey everything I have commanded you.

242. What does it mean to baptize "in the name of the Father and of the Son and of the Holy Spirit"?

It means that in Baptism, God, the Holy Trinity, receives me into communion or fellowship with Himself.

243. Who is to baptize?

Normally the called ministers of Christ are to baptize,

but in cases of emergency and when no pastor is available, any Christian should baptize.

834　　**1 Cor. 4:1** Let a man so consider us, as servants of Christ and stewards of the mysteries of God (NKJV).

Note: For a short form of Baptism in cases of emergency, see the end of this section.

244. Who is to be baptized?

"All nations" are to be baptized, that is, all people, young and old.

245. What distinction is to be made in baptizing?

A. Those who can receive instruction are to be baptized after they have been instructed in the main articles of the Christian faith.

835　　**Acts 2:38–39** Peter replied, "Repent and be baptized, every one of you, in the name of Jesus Christ for the forgiveness of your sins. And you will receive the gift of the Holy Spirit. The promise is for you and your children and for all who are far off—for all whom the Lord our God will call."

836　　**Acts 2:41** Those who accepted his message were baptized.

Bible narratives: The Ethiopian was instructed before he was baptized **(Acts 8:26–39).** The jailer was instructed before he was baptized **(Acts 16:25–33).**

B. Little children should be baptized when they are brought to Baptism by those who have authority over them.

837　　**Mark 10:13–15** People were bringing little children to Jesus to have Him touch them, but the disciples rebuked them. When Jesus saw this, He was indignant. He said to them, "Let the little children come to Me, and do not hinder them, for the kingdom of God belongs to such as these. I tell you the truth, anyone who will not receive the kingdom of God like a little child will never enter it."

246. Why are babies to be baptized?

Babies are to be baptized because

A. they are included in the words "all nations";

838   **Matt. 28:19** Go and make disciples of all nations, baptizing them in the name of the Father and of the Son and of the Holy Spirit.

839   **Acts 2:38–39** Repent and be baptized, every one of you, in the name of Jesus Christ for the forgiveness of your sins. And you will receive the gift of the Holy Spirit. The promise is for you and your children.

B. Jesus especially invites little children to come to Him;

840   **Luke 18:15–17** People were also bringing babies to Jesus to have Him touch them. When the disciples saw this, they rebuked them. But Jesus called the children to Him and said, "Let the little children come to Me, and do not hinder them, for the kingdom of God belongs to such as these. I tell you the truth, anyone who will not receive the kingdom of God like a little child, will never enter it."

C. as sinners, babies need what Baptism offers;

841   **John 3:5–6** No one can enter the kingdom of God unless he is born of water and the Spirit. Flesh gives birth to flesh, but the Spirit gives birth to spirit.

842   **Eph. 2:3** Like the rest, we were by nature objects of wrath.

D. babies also are able to have faith.

843   **Matt. 18:6** If anyone causes one of these little ones
       who believe in Me to sin, it would be better for him
       to have a large millstone hung around his neck and
       to be drowned in the depths of the sea.

Bible narrative: John the Baptist was "filled with the
Holy Spirit even from birth" **(Luke 1:15),** and even
before birth **(1:41–44).**

**247. Why does the church encourage the use of
sponsors at Baptisms?**

Sponsors witness that those who receive this sacrament have been properly baptized. They also pray for
them and in the case of children, help with their Christian upbringing, especially if they should lose their parents. Only those of the same confession of faith should
be sponsors.

844   **Matt. 18:16** "Every matter may be established by
       the testimony of two or three witnesses."

845   **Eph. 4:16** From Him the whole body, joined and
       held together by every supporting ligament, grows
       and builds itself up in love, as each part does its
       work.

II. The Blessings of Baptism

Second

What benefits does Baptism give?

It works forgiveness of sins, rescues from death
and the devil, and gives eternal salvation to all who
believe this, as the words and promises of God
declare.

Which are these words and promises of God?

Christ our Lord says in the last chapter of Mark: "Whoever believes and is baptized will be saved, but whoever does not believe will be condemned." **[Mark 16:16]**

248. What great and precious things are given in Baptism?

Baptism

A. works forgiveness of sins;

846   **Acts 2:38** Repent and be baptized, every one of you, in the name of Jesus Christ for the forgiveness of your sins.

847   **Acts 22:16** Get up, be baptized and wash your sins away.

B. rescues from death and the devil;

848   **Rom. 6:3, 5** Don't you know that all of us who were baptized into Christ Jesus were baptized into His death? . . . If we have been united with Him like this in His death, we will certainly also be united with Him in His resurrection.

849   **Gal. 3:27** All of you who were baptized into Christ have clothed yourselves with Christ.

850   **Col. 1:13–14** He has rescued us from the dominion of darkness and brought us into the kingdom of the Son He loves, in whom we have redemption, the forgiveness of sins. (Compare **Col. 2:11–12.**)

C. gives eternal salvation.

851   **Mark 16:16** Whoever believes and is baptized will be saved.

852   **1 Peter 3:21** This water [of Noah's flood] symbolizes baptism that now saves you also. . . . It saves you by the resurrection of Jesus Christ.

853   **Titus 3:5** He saved us through the washing of
        rebirth and renewal by the Holy Spirit.

*249. If Christ has already won forgiveness and sal-
vation for us and gives us all this by grace alone, why
do we still need Baptism?*

Christ has indeed won full forgiveness and salvation
for the whole human race with His perfect life, suffering,
death, and resurrection. He distributes this same
forgiveness in Baptism. (Baptism is a means of grace.)

854   **1 Cor. 6:11** You were washed, you were sanctified,
        you were justified in the name of the Lord Jesus
        Christ and by the Spirit of our God.

855   **Titus 3:5–7** He saved us through the washing of
        rebirth and renewal by the Holy Spirit, whom He
        poured out on us generously through Jesus Christ
        our Savior, so that, having been justified by His
        grace, we might become heirs having the hope of
        eternal life.

250. To whom does Baptism give all these blessings?

Baptism gives these blessings to all who believe
God's saving promises.

856   **Mark 16:16** Whoever believes and is baptized will
        be saved, but whoever does not believe will be
        condemned.

*251. Is it possible for an unbaptized person to be
saved?*

It is only unbelief that condemns. Faith cannot exist
in the heart of a person who despises and rejects
Baptism against better knowledge. But those who
believe the Gospel, yet die before they have opportunity
to be baptized are not condemned.

857   **Mark 16:16** Whoever does not believe will be condemned.

Bible narratives: The Pharisees and experts in the Law in unbelief rejected John's baptism **(Luke 7:30).** The thief on the cross was saved without Baptism **(Luke 23:39–43).**

252. Why are we not to seek a "baptism with the Holy Spirit" in addition to the Sacrament of Holy Baptism?

Beyond sacramental Baptism we are to seek no other "baptism" because

A. there is no other God-given Baptism today beside the Sacrament of Holy Baptism;

858   **Eph. 4:5** One Lord, one faith, one baptism.

Note: The "instruction about baptisms" **(Heb. 6:2)** does not mean that there are several Christian baptisms, but that the one true Baptism must be clearly distinguished from the many religious washings which were common in the ancient world (see for instance **Mark 7:4**).

B. the sacrament is not a water-only or a Spirit-only baptism, but a water-and-Spirit Baptism;

859   **John 3:5** No one can enter the kingdom of God unless he is born of water and the Spirit.

860   **Titus 3:5** He saved us through the washing of rebirth and renewal by the Holy Spirit.

Note: **Matt. 3:11** speaks of baptizing "with water" and "with the Holy Spirit and with fire." The difference here is not between sacramental Baptism and some sort of "Spirit baptism," but between the preparatory mission and baptism of John the Baptist and the full, permanent mission and Baptism of Jesus Christ. While John's baptism also gave the forgiveness of sins, it was different in that it pointed forward to the redemptive work of the Savior.

C. the special signs granted by the Holy Spirit were not another "baptism," but they proved the truth and power of the apostles' preaching.

861   **Acts 19:6** When Paul placed his hands on them, the Holy Spirit came on them and they spoke in tongues and prophesied.

862   **2 Cor. 12:12** The things that mark an apostle—signs, wonders and miracles—were done among you with great perseverance.

Note: See question 164.

III. The Power of Baptism

Third

How can water do such great things?

Certainly not just water, but the word of God in and with the water does these things, along with the faith which trusts this word of God in the water. For without God's word the water is plain water and no Baptism. But with the word of God it is a Baptism, that is, a life-giving water, rich in grace, and a washing of the new birth in the Holy Spirit, as St. Paul says in Titus chapter three:

"He saved us through the washing of rebirth and renewal by the Holy Spirit, whom He poured out on us generously through Jesus Christ our Savior, so that, having been justified by His grace, we might become heirs having the hope of eternal life. This is a trustworthy saying." **[Titus 3:5–8]**

253. How does baptismal water work forgiveness of sins, rescue from death and the devil, and give eternal salvation?

God's words of institution put these great blessings into Baptism. Faith, which trusts this word of God in the water, takes the blessings out and makes them our own.

863   **Eph. 5:26** Christ loved the church and gave Himself up for her to make her holy, cleansing her by the washing with water through the word.

864   **Gal. 3:26–27** You are all sons of God through faith in Christ Jesus, for all of you who were baptized into Christ have clothed yourselves with Christ.

254. Why do the Scriptures call Baptism the washing of rebirth and renewal of the Holy Spirit?

In Baptism, the Holy Spirit works faith and so creates in us new spiritual life with the power to overcome sin.

865   **Rom. 6:6** Our old man was crucified with Him, that the body of sin might be done away with, that we should no longer be slaves of sin (NKJV).

866   **Titus 3:5–8** He saved us through the washing of rebirth and renewal of the Holy Spirit, whom He poured out on us generously through Jesus Christ our Savior, so that, having been justified by His grace, we might become heirs having the hope of eternal life. This is a trustworthy saying.

IV. What Baptism Indicates

Fourth

What does such baptizing with water indicate?

It indicates that the Old Adam in us should by daily contrition and repentance be drowned and die with all sins and evil desires, and that a new man should daily emerge and arise to live before God in righteousness and purity forever.

Where is this written?

St. Paul writes in Romans chapter six: "We were therefore buried with Him through baptism into death in order that, just as Christ was raised from the dead through the glory of the Father, we too may live a new life." **[Rom. 6:4]**

255. What is the Old Adam?

The Old Adam is the corrupt and evil nature that we inherit because of Adam's fall into sin.

867   **Eph. 4:22** Put off, concerning your former conduct, the old man which grows corrupt according to the deceitful lusts (NKJV).

256. How is this Old Adam to be drowned in us?

The Old Adam is to be drowned by daily contrition (sorrow for sins) and repentance (faith), by which we resist and overcome evil desires.

868   **Luke 9:23** If anyone would come after Me, he must deny himself and take up his cross daily and follow Me.

869   **Gal. 5:24** Those who belong to Christ Jesus have

crucified the sinful nature with its passions and desires.

257. What is the new man?

The new man is the new spiritual life and nature, created in us by the washing of rebirth.

870   **2 Cor. 5:17** If anyone is in Christ, he is a new creation.

258. How is this new man to emerge and arise?

The new man emerges and arises as we daily live and grow before God in true faith and good works.

871   **Eph. 4:24** Put on the new man which was created according to God, in righteousness and true holiness (NKJV).

259. How does Baptism indicate the daily drowning of the Old Adam and the emergence of the new man?

By Baptism we have been made to share in Christ's death and resurrection. As He has buried our sin, so we too can and must daily overcome and bury it. And as He is risen from the dead and lives, so we too can and must daily live a new life in Him.

872   **Rom. 6:3–4** Don't you know that all of us who were baptized into Christ Jesus were baptized into His death? We were therefore buried with Him through baptism into death in order that, just as Christ was raised from the dead through the glory of the Father, we too may live a new life.

260. With which words do we regularly remember our Baptism?

The words "in the name of the Father, and of the Son, and of the Holy Spirit" come from the baptismal command **(Matt. 28:19)** and are known as the Trinitarian Invocation. By repeating these words, in church or by ourselves, we recall, claim, and confess before heaven, earth, and hell all that God the Holy Trinity has given us in our Baptism.

873   **Rom. 8:38–39** I am convinced that neither death nor life, neither angels nor demons, neither the present nor the future, nor any powers, neither height nor depth, nor anything else in all creation, will be able to separate us from the love of God that is in Christ Jesus our Lord.

Bible narrative: The three persons of the blessed Trinity revealed themselves at the Baptism of our Lord **(Luke 3:21–22).**

Note: The Trinitarian Invocation may be accompanied by the sign of the cross, made at our Baptism upon our foreheads and hearts to mark us as "redeemed by Christ the crucified."

A Short Form for Holy Baptism in Cases of Emergency

In urgent cases, in the absence of a pastor, any Christian may administer Holy Baptism. Take water, call the person by name, and apply the water, saying: "I baptize you in the name of the Father and of the Son and of the Holy Spirit. Amen."

If there is time, Baptism may be preceded by the Apostles' Creed and the Lord's Prayer.

CONFESSION

"When I urge you to go to confession, I am simply urging you to be a Christian."

(Large Catechism, Brief Exhortation 32)

What is confession?

Confession has two parts.

First that we confess our sins, and

second, that we receive absolution, that is, forgiveness, from the pastor as from God Himself, not doubting, but firmly believing that by it our sins are forgiven before God in heaven.

What sins should we confess?

Before God we should plead guilty of all sins, even those we are not aware of, as we do in the Lord's

Prayer; but before the pastor we should confess only those sins which we know and feel in our hearts.

Which are these?

Consider your place in life according to the Ten Commandments: Are you a father, mother, son, daughter, husband, wife, or worker? Have you been disobedient, unfaithful, or lazy? Have you been hot-tempered, rude, or quarrelsome? Have you hurt someone by your words or deeds? Have you stolen, been negligent, wasted anything, or done any harm?

261. What is the first part of confession?

The first part of confession is that we confess, or acknowledge, our sins.

874 **Ps. 32:3, 5** When I kept silent, my bones wasted away through my groaning all day long. . . . Then I acknowledged my sin to You and did not cover up my iniquity. I said, "I will confess my transgressions to the Lord"—and You forgave the guilt of my sin.

875 **Ps. 51:1–4** Have mercy on me, O God, according to Your unfailing love; according to Your great compassion blot out my transgressions. Wash away all my iniquity and cleanse me from my sin. For I know my transgressions, and my sin is always before me. Against You, You only, have I sinned and done what is evil in Your sight, that You are proved right when You speak and justified when You judge.

262. What sins should we confess before God?

Before God we should plead guilty of all sins, even those we are not aware of, as we do in the Lord's Prayer.

876   **Ps. 19:12** Who can discern his errors? Forgive my hidden faults.

877   **Prov. 28:13** He who conceals his sins does not prosper, but whoever confesses and renounces them finds mercy.

878   **1 John 1:8–9** If we claim to be without sin, we deceive ourselves and the truth is not in us. If we confess our sins, He is faithful and just and will forgive us our sins and purify us from all unrighteousness.

263. What sins should we confess before our neighbor?

Before our neighbor we should confess all sins we have committed against him or her.

879   **James 5:16** Confess your sins to each other.

880   **Matt. 5:23–24** If you are offering your gift at the altar and there remember that your brother has something against you, leave your gift there in front of the altar. First go and be reconciled to your brother; then come and offer your gift.

264. What sins are we encouraged to confess privately before our pastor or confessor?

Before the pastor or confessor we confess those sins which we know and feel in our hearts, especially those that trouble us.

881   **2 Sam. 12:13** David said to Nathan, "I have sinned against the Lord." Nathan replied, "The Lord has taken away your sin."

882   **James 5:16** Confess your sins to each other and pray for each other so that you may be healed.

Note: No one may be forced to make private confession.

265. What is the second part of confession?

The second part of confession is that we receive absolution, that is, forgiveness of sins.

883   **Is. 1:18** "Come now, let us reason together," says the Lord. "Though your sins are like scarlet, they shall be as white as snow; though they are red as crimson, they shall be like wool."

266. How should we regard the absolution (forgiveness) spoken by the pastor?

We should receive the pastor's absolution as from God Himself, not doubting, but firmly believing that by it our sins are forgiven before God in heaven.

"It is not the voice or word of the man who speaks it, but it is the Word of God, who forgives sin, for it is spoken in God's stead and by God's command" (Augsburg Confession XXV 3).

884   **Matt. 18:18** Whatever you loose on earth will be loosed in heaven.

885   **Luke 10:16** He who listens to you listens to Me.

886   **John 20:23** If you forgive anyone his sins, they are forgiven.

267. What assurance do I have that my private confession to the pastor will remain confidential?

The pastor is pledged not to tell anyone else of sins told him in private confession, for those sins have been removed.

887   **Ps. 103:12** As far as the east is from the west, so far has He removed our transgressions from us.

888   **Prov. 11:13** A gossip betrays a confidence, but a trustworthy man keeps a secret.

889   **1 Tim. 3:1–2** Here is a trustworthy saying: If

anyone sets his heart on being an overseer [pastor], he desires a noble task. Now the overseer must be above reproach.

268. What is the benefit of private confession and absolution?

In private confession and absolution, God Himself through the pastor forgives each individual the sins that are confessed.

"If there is a heart that feels its sin and desires consolation, it has here a sure refuge when it hears in God's Word that through a man God looses and absolves him from his sins" (Large Catechism, Brief Exhortation 14).

890 **Ps. 32:2** Blessed is the man whose sin the Lord does not count against him.

891 **2 Sam. 12:13** Nathan replied, "The Lord has taken away your sin."

892 **Matt. 9:2** Take heart, son; your sins are forgiven.

A Short Form of Confession

[Luther intended the following form to serve only as an example of private confession for Christians of his time. For a contemporary form of individual confession, see *Lutheran Worship*, pp. 310–11.]

The penitent says:

Dear confessor, I ask you please to hear my confession and to pronounce forgiveness in order to fulfill God's will.

I, a poor sinner, plead guilty before God of all sins. In particular I confess before you that as a servant, maid, etc., I, sad to say, serve my master unfaithfully, for in this and that I have not done what I was told to do. I have made him angry and caused him to curse. I have been negligent and allowed damage to be done. I have also been offensive in words and deeds. I have quarreled with my peers. I have grumbled about the lady of the house and cursed her. I am sorry for all of this and I ask for grace. I want to do better.

A master or lady of the house may say:

In particular I confess before you that I have not faithfully guided my children, servants, and wife to the glory of God. I have cursed. I have set a bad example by indecent words and deeds. I have hurt my neighbor and spoken evil of him. I have over-charged, sold inferior merchandise, and given less than was paid for.

[Let the penitent confess whatever else he has done against God's commandments and his own position.]

If, however, someone does not find himself burdened with these or greater sins, he should not trouble himself or search for or invent other sins, and thereby make confession a torture. Instead, he should mention one or two that he knows: In particular I confess that I have cursed; I have used improper words; I have neglected this or that, etc. Let that be enough.

But if you know of none at all (which hardly seems possible), then mention none in particular, but receive the forgiveness upon the general confession which you make to God before the confessor.

Then the confessor shall say:

God be merciful to you and strengthen your faith. Amen.

Furthermore:

Do you believe that my forgiveness is God's forgiveness?

Yes, dear confessor.

Then let him say:

Let it be done for you as you believe. And I, by the command of our Lord Jesus Christ, forgive you your sins in the name of the Father and of the Son and of the Holy Spirit. Amen. Go in peace.

A confessor will know additional passages with which to comfort and to strengthen the faith of those who have great burdens of conscience or are sorrowful and distressed.

This is intended only as a general form of confession.

The Office of the Keys

What is the Office of the Keys?

The Office of the Keys is that special authority which Christ has given to His church on earth to forgive the sins of repentant sinners, but to withhold forgiveness from the unrepentant as long as they do not repent.

Where is this written?

This is what St. John the Evangelist writes in chapter twenty: The Lord Jesus breathed on His disciples and said, "Receive the Holy Spirit. If you forgive anyone his sins, they are forgiven; if you do not forgive them, they are not forgiven." **[John 20:22–23]**

What do you believe according to these words?

I believe that when the called ministers of Christ deal with us by His divine command, in particular when they exclude openly unrepentant sinners from the Christian congregation and absolve those who repent of their sins and want to do better, this is just as valid and certain, even in heaven, as if Christ our dear Lord dealt with us Himself.

269. What special authority has Christ given to His church on earth?

Christ has given to His church the authority to forgive sins or to withhold forgiveness.

893   **Matt. 18:18** I tell you the truth, whatever you bind on earth will be bound in heaven, and whatever you loose on earth will be loosed in heaven.

894   **John 20:22–23** [Jesus] breathed on them and said, "Receive the Holy Spirit. If you forgive anyone his sins, they are forgiven; if you do not forgive them, they are not forgiven."

270. Why is this authority called the Office of the Keys?

This authority works like a key to open heaven by forgiving sins, or to close heaven by not forgiving them.

895   **Matt. 16:19** I will give you the keys of the kingdom of heaven.

271. How is the Office of the Keys related to the proclamation of the Gospel?

The Office of the Keys is a special God-given way of applying the Gospel to the individual. "God is surpassingly rich in His grace: First, through the spoken word, by which the forgiveness of sin (the peculiar function of the Gospel) is preached to the whole world; second, through Baptism; third, through the holy Sacrament of the Altar; fourth, through the power of keys; and finally, through the mutual conversation and consolation of brethren" (Smalcald Articles III IV).

896   **Matt. 18:20** Where two or three come together in My name, there am I with them.

897   **Matt. 28:18–20** Jesus came to them and said, "All authority in heaven and on earth has been given to Me. Therefore go and make disciples of all nations, baptizing them in the name of the Father and of the Son and of the Holy Spirit, and teaching them to obey everything I have commanded you. And surely I am with you always, to the very end of the age."

898   **1 Peter 2:9** You are a chosen people, a royal priesthood, a holy nation, a people belonging to God, that you may declare the praises of Him who called you out of darkness into His wonderful light.

272. Who are to be forgiven (absolved)?

Those who repent and ask for forgiveness are to be forgiven.

899   **Acts 3:19** Repent, then, and turn to God, so that your sins may be wiped out, that times of refreshing may come from the Lord.

273. Who receives the forgiveness given in absolution?

Only repentant believers receive the forgiveness.

900   **Ps. 32:5** I acknowledged my sin to You and did not cover up my iniquity. I said, "I will confess my transgressions to the Lord"—and You forgave the guilt of my sin.

274. Who are repentant believers?

Repentant believers are those who are sorry for their sins (contrition) and believe in the Lord Jesus Christ as their Savior (faith).

901   **Ps. 51:17** The sacrifices of God are a broken spirit; a broken and contrite heart, O God, You will not despise.

902   **Acts 16:31** Believe in the Lord Jesus, and you will be saved.

Note: Secretly unrepentant sinners (hypocrites) reject the forgiveness which the absolution truly offers them.

275. Who are not to be forgiven?

Unrepentant sinners, that is, those who are not sorry

for their sins and do not believe in Jesus Christ, are not to be forgiven as long as they do not repent.

903   **Matt. 18:17** If he refuses to listen to them, tell it to the church; and if he refuses to listen even to the church, treat him as you would a pagan or a tax collector.

276. What is the necessary result of repentance?

"Then good works, which are the fruits of repentance, are bound to follow" (Augsburg Confession XII 6).

904   **Matt. 3:8** Produce fruit in keeping with repentance.
905   **John 8:11** Go now and leave your life of sin.

Bible narrative: Zacchaeus the tax collector **(Luke 19:1–10).**

277. How does the church publicly exercise the Office of the Keys?

The Christian congregation by the command of Christ calls pastors to carry out the Office of the Keys publicly in His name and on behalf of the congregation. The pastoral office is a divine institution.

906   **Eph. 4:11** It was He [Christ] who gave some to be apostles, some to be prophets, some to be evangelists, and some to be pastors and teachers.

907   **Acts 20:28** Keep watch over yourselves and all the flock of which the Holy Spirit has made you overseers.

908   **1 Cor. 4:1** Let a man so consider us, as servants of Christ and stewards of the mysteries of God (NKJV).

909   **2 Cor. 2:10** What I have forgiven . . . I have forgiven in the sight of Christ for your sake.

278. Who should be considered for the office of pastor?

Congregations are to call men who are well qualified personally and spiritually to be their pastors.

"Our churches teach that nobody should preach publicly in the church or administer the sacraments unless he is regularly called" (Augsburg Confession XIV).

910   **1 Tim. 3:1–2** If anyone sets his heart on being an overseer [pastor], he desires a noble task. Now the overseer must be above reproach, the husband of but one wife, temperate, self-controlled, respectable, hospitable, able to teach.

911   **2 Tim. 2:2** The things you have heard me say in the presence of many witnesses entrust to reliable men who will also be qualified to teach others.

912   **2 Tim. 2:15** Do your best to present yourself to God as one approved, a workman who does not need to be ashamed and who correctly handles the word of truth.

913   **1 Cor. 14:33–34** As in all the congregations of the saints, women should remain silent in the churches. They are not allowed to speak, but must be in submission, as the Law says.

Note: See also **1 Tim. 2:11–14.**

Church Discipline and Excommunication

279. What great care must be taken in dealing with an openly unrepentant sinner?

The Christian congregation must carry out church discipline in love and patience. "If your brother sins against you, go and show him his fault, just between the two of you. If he listens to you, you have won your brother over. But if he will not listen take one or two others along, so that 'every matter may be established by the testimony of two or three witnesses.' If he refuses to listen to them, tell it to the church; and if he refuses to listen even to the church, treat him as you would a pagan or a tax collector" **(Matt. 18:15–17).**

914   **Gal. 6:1–2** Brothers, if someone is caught in a sin, you who are spiritual should restore him gently. But watch yourself, or you also may be tempted. Carry each other's burdens, and in this way you will fulfill the law of Christ.

915   **Eph. 4:2–3** Be completely humble and gentle; be patient, bearing with one another in love. Make every effort to keep the unity of the Spirit through the bond of peace.

280. What must the congregation finally do with openly unrepentant sinners?

The Christian congregation must exclude openly unrepentant sinners (excommunication).

916   **1 Cor. 5:13** God will judge those outside. "Expel the wicked man from among you."

281. By what authority does the congregation excommunicate openly unrepentant sinners?

Excommunication is authorized by Christ and is just as valid and certain, even in heaven, as if Christ our dear Lord dealt with us Himself.

917   **Matt. 18:18** I tell you the truth, whatever you bind on earth will be bound in heaven.

282. What is the duty of the called minister of Christ when the congregation has excommunicated a sinner?

The called minister of Christ must carry out the resolution of the congregation, that is, he must exclude the excommunicated person from the rights and privileges of a Christian.

283. What is the purpose of excommunication?

Excommunication is not intended to punish the sinner, but to

A. lead him or her to repentance and faith;

918   **Matt. 12:20** A bruised reed He will not break, and a smoldering wick He will not snuff out.

919   **Acts 3:19** Repent, then, and turn to God, so that your sins may be wiped out.

B. prevent him or her from leading others into sin.

921   **Matt. 18:6** If anyone causes one of these little ones who believe in Me to sin, it would be better for him to have a large millstone hung around his neck and to be drowned in the depths of the sea.

922   **1 Cor. 5:6** Your boasting is not good. Don't you know that a little yeast works through the whole batch of dough?

284. What is the duty of a congregation toward an excommunicated sinner who repents?

The congregation must forgive any excommunicated person who repents and receive him or her back into full fellowship.

923   **2 Cor. 2:7–8** Now instead, you ought to forgive and comfort him so that he will not be overwhelmed by excessive sorrow. I urge you, therefore, to reaffirm your love for him.

THE SACRAMENT
OF THE ALTAR

I. The Nature of the Sacrament of the Altar

What is the Sacrament of the Altar?

It is the true body and blood of our Lord Jesus Christ under the bread and wine, instituted by Christ Himself for us Christians to eat and to drink.

Where is this written?

The holy Evangelists Matthew, Mark, Luke, and St. Paul write:

Our Lord Jesus Christ, on the night when He was betrayed, took bread, and when He had given thanks, He broke it and gave it to the disciples and said: "Take, eat; this is My body, which is given for you. This do in remembrance of Me."

In the same way also He took the cup after supper, and when He had given thanks, He gave it to them, saying, "Drink of it, all of you; this cup is the new testament in My blood, which is shed for you for the forgiveness of sins. This do, as often as you drink it, in remembrance of Me."

285. What are some other names for the Sacrament of the Altar?

This sacrament is also called the Lord's Supper, the Lord's Table, Holy Communion, the Breaking of Bread, and the Eucharist.

924   **1 Cor. 11:20** When you come together, it is not the Lord's Supper you eat.

925   **1 Cor. 10:21** You cannot have a part in both the Lord's table and the table of demons.

926   **1 Cor. 10:16** The cup of blessing which we bless, is it not the communion of the blood of Christ? The bread which we break, is it not the communion of the body of Christ? (NKJV).

927   **Acts 2:42** They devoted themselves to the apostles' teaching and to the fellowship, to the breaking of bread and to prayer.

928   **Matt. 26:26** Jesus took bread, gave thanks and broke it, and gave it to His disciples, saying, "Take and eat; this is My body."

Note: Eucharist comes from the Greek word for "giving thanks."

286. Who instituted the Sacrament of the Altar?

Jesus Christ, who is true God and true man, instituted this sacrament.

929   **1 Cor. 11:23–24** I received from the Lord what I also passed on to you: The Lord Jesus, on the night He was betrayed, took bread, and when He had given thanks, He broke it and said, "This is My body, which is for you; do this in remembrance of Me."

287. What does Christ give us in this sacrament?

In this sacrament Christ gives us His own true body and blood for the forgiveness of sins.

930   **Matt. 26:26, 28** "This is My body. . . . This is My blood."

288. How does the Bible make it clear that these words of Christ are not picture language?

Christ's words in the Sacrament must be taken at face value especially because

A. these words are the words of a testament, and even an ordinary person's last will and testament may not be changed once that person has died;

931   **1 Cor. 11:25** "This cup is the new covenant [testament] in My blood."

932   **Gal. 3:15** Though it is only a man's covenant [will], yet if it is confirmed, no one annuls or adds to it (NKJV).

Note: Compare also **Heb. 9:15–22**.

B. God's Word clearly teaches that in the Sacrament the bread and wine are a communion or participation in the body and blood of Christ;

933   **1 Cor. 10:16** The cup of blessing which we bless, is
           it not the communion of the blood of Christ? The
           bread which we break, is it not the communion of
           the body of Christ? (NKJV).

C. God's Word clearly teaches that those who misuse
the Sacrament sin not against bread and wine but
against Christ's body and blood.

934   **1 Cor. 11:27, 29** Whoever eats the bread or drinks
           the cup of the Lord in an unworthy manner will be
           guilty of sinning against the body and blood of the
           Lord. . . . For anyone who eats and drinks without
           recognizing the body of the Lord eats and drinks
           judgment on himself.

289. What are the visible elements in the Sacrament?

The visible elements are bread and wine.

935   **Matt. 26:26–27** Jesus took bread. . . . Then He took
           the cup.

Note: "The fruit of the vine" **(Luke 22:18)** in the
Bible means wine, not grape juice. See also **1 Cor.
11:21.**

*290. Do Christ's body and blood in the Sacrament
replace the bread and wine, so that the bread and wine
are no longer there?*

No, bread and wine remain in the Sacrament.

936   **1 Cor. 11:26** Whenever you eat this bread and
           drink this cup, you proclaim the Lord's death until
           He comes.

*291. How then are the bread and wine in the
Sacrament the body and blood of Christ?*

The bread and wine in the Sacrament are Christ's

body and blood by sacramental union. By the power of His word, Christ gives His body and blood in, with, and under the consecrated (blessed) bread and wine.

937   **1 Cor. 10:16** The cup of blessing which we bless, is it not the communion of the blood of Christ? The bread which we break, is it not the communion of the body of Christ? (NKJV).

292. Do all communicants receive the body and blood in the Sacrament, whether or not they believe?

Yes, because the Sacrament depends on Christ's word, not on our faith.

938   **1 Cor. 11:27** Whoever eats the bread or drinks the cup of the Lord in an unworthy manner will be guilty of sinning against the body and blood of the Lord.

Note: All communicants should receive both parts of the Sacrament, since Christ said, "Take and eat; this is my body. . . . Drink from it, all of you" **(Matt. 26:26–27).**

293. Are the body and blood of Christ in the Sacrament sacrificed again to God for the sins of the living and the dead?

No, the body and blood of Christ in the Sacrament are the one perfect sacrifice offered to God once and for all on the cross and are now distributed to us in the Sacrament together with all the blessings and benefits which this sacrifice has won for us.

939   **1 Cor. 5:7** Christ, our Passover lamb, has been sacrificed.

940   **Heb. 10:14** By one sacrifice He has made perfect forever those who are being made holy.

941 **Heb. 10:18** Where these [sins] have been forgiven, there is no longer any sacrifice for sin.

Note: We speak of the "Sacrament of the Altar" because an altar is a place of sacrifice. Jesus sacrificed His body and blood on the cross for the sins of the world once and for all. In the Sacrament of the Altar, He distributes this same body and blood until the end of time.

294. What does Christ command when He says, "This do in remembrance of Me"?

Christ commands in these words that His Sacrament be celebrated in the church till the end of time as a living proclamation and distribution of His saving death and all its blessings.

942 **1 Cor. 11:26** Whenever you eat this bread and drink this cup, you proclaim the Lord's death until He comes.

295. Why are we to receive the Sacrament often?

We are to receive the Sacrament often because

A. Christ commands, or urgently invites, us, saying, "This do in remembrance of Me";

B. His words, "Given and shed for you for the forgiveness of sins" promise and offer us great blessings;

943 **Matt. 11:28** Come to Me, all you who are weary and burdened and I will give you rest.

C. we need the forgiveness of our sins and the strength for a new and holy life.

944 **John 15:5** I am the vine; you are the branches. If a man remains in Me and I in him, he will bear much fruit; apart from Me you can do nothing.

Note: In the New Testament, the Sacrament was a regular and major feature of congregational worship, not an occasional extra **(Acts 2:42; 20:7; 1 Cor. 11:20, 33).** In Reformation times our churches celebrated the Sacrament "every Sunday and on other festivals" (Apology XXIV 1).

II. The Benefit of the Sacrament of the Altar

What is the benefit of this eating and drinking?

These words, "Given and shed for you for the forgiveness of sins," show us that in the Sacrament forgiveness of sins, life, and salvation are given us through these words. For where there is forgiveness of sins, there is also life and salvation.

296. What is the benefit offered in the sacrament?

A. The chief blessing of the Sacrament is the forgiveness of sins which Christ's body and blood have won for us on the cross. (The Lord's Supper is a means of grace.)

945   **Matt. 26:28** This is My blood of the covenant, which is poured out for many for the forgiveness of sins.

946   **1 Peter 1:18–19** You know that it was not with perishable things such as silver or gold that you were redeemed from the empty way of life handed down to you from your forefathers, but with the precious blood of Christ, a lamb without blemish or defect.

947   **Col. 1:22** He has reconciled you by Christ's physical body through death to present you holy in His sight, without blemish and free from accusation.

948   **1 John 1:7** The blood of Jesus, His Son, purifies us from all sin.

B. Together with forgiveness, God gives all other blessings as well, that is, "life and salvation."

"We must never regard the sacrament as a harmful thing from which we should flee, but as a pure, wholesome, soothing medicine which aids and quickens us in both soul and body. For where the soul is healed, the body has benefited also" (Large Catechism V 68).

"We are talking about the presence of the living Christ, knowing that 'death no longer has dominion over Him' " **[Rom. 6:9]** (Apology X 4).

949   **Rom. 6:8–9** If we died with Christ, we believe that we will also live with Him. For we know that since Christ was raised from the dead, He cannot die again; death no longer has mastery over Him.

950   **Rom. 8:31–32** If God is for us, who can be against us? He who did not spare His own Son, but gave Him up for us all—how will He not also, along with Him, graciously give us all things?

C. In the Sacrament Christ gives victory over sin and hell and strength for the new life in Him.

951   **Rom. 8:10** If Christ is in you, your body is dead because of sin, yet your spirit is alive because of righteousness.

952   **1 Peter 2:24** He Himself bore our sins in His body on the tree, so that we might die to sins and live for righteousness; by His wounds you have been healed.

D. As Christians partake of this sacrament together, they make a solemn public confession of Christ and of unity in the truth of His Gospel.

953   **1 Cor. 10:17** Because there is one loaf, we, who are many, are one body, for we all partake of the one loaf.

954   **1 Cor. 11:26** Whenever you eat this bread and drink this cup, you proclaim the Lord's death until He comes.

Note: See also **Heb. 12:22–24.**

III. The Power of the Sacrament of the Altar

How can bodily eating and drinking do such great things?

Certainly not just eating and drinking do these things, but the words written here: "Given and shed for you for the forgiveness of sins." These words, along with the bodily eating and drinking, are the main thing in the Sacrament. Whoever believes these words has exactly what they say: "forgiveness of sins."

297. How can forgiveness, life, and salvation be obtained through bodily eating and drinking?

Not simply the eating and drinking, but the words of Christ together with His body and blood under the bread and wine are the way through which these blessings are given. "We do not claim this of bread and wine—since in itself bread is bread—but of that bread and wine which are Christ's body and blood and with which the words are coupled. These and no other, we say, are the treasure through which forgiveness is obtained" (Large Catechism V 28). Christ's words of promise have put these gifts into the Sacrament, and the believer receives them there through faith.

298. Does everyone who eats and drinks the Sacrament also receive forgiveness, life, and salvation?

Forgiveness, life, and salvation are truly offered to all who eat the Lord's body and blood in the Sacrament, but only through faith can we receive the blessings offered there.

955   **Luke 1:45** Blessed is she who has believed that what the Lord has said to her will be accomplished.

956   **Luke 11:27–28** "Blessed is the mother who gave you birth and nursed you." He replied: "Blessed rather are those who hear the word of God and obey it."

Note: To "keep" or "obey" God's Word of promise is to believe or trust it. "For in the Gospel a righteousness from God is revealed, a righteousness that is by faith from first to last, just as it is written: 'The righteous will live by faith'" **(Rom. 1:17)**.

957   **1 Cor. 10:3–5** They all ate the same spiritual food and drank the same spiritual drink; for they drank from the spiritual rock that accompanied them, and that rock was Christ. Nevertheless, God was not pleased with most of them; their bodies were scattered over the desert.

Bible narrative: There was a blessing in touching Jesus or being touched by Him, and faith received it **(Matt. 9:20–22, 27–29)**.

IV. How to Receive This Sacrament Worthily

Who receives this sacrament worthily?

Fasting and bodily preparation are certainly fine outward training. But that person is truly worthy and well prepared who has faith in these words: "Given and shed for you for the forgiveness of sins."

But anyone who does not believe these words or doubts them is unworthy and unprepared, for the words "for you" require all hearts to believe.

299. Why is it important to receive the Sacrament worthily?

It is very important because St. Paul clearly teaches: "Whoever eats the bread or drinks the cup of the Lord in an unworthy manner will be guilty of sinning against the body and blood of the Lord. A man ought to examine himself before he eats of the bread and drinks of the cup. For anyone who eats and drinks without recognizing the body of the Lord eats and drinks judgment on himself" **(1 Cor. 11:27–29).**

300. Is it necessary to fast before receiving the Sacrament?

Fasting can be good training for the will, but God does not command particular times, places, and forms for this.

958   **1 Tim. 4:8** Physical training is of some value, but godliness has value for all things.

Note: See also **1 Cor. 9:24–27.**

301. When do we receive the Sacrament worthily?

We receive it worthily when we have faith in Christ and His words, "Given and shed for you for the forgiveness of sins."

302. When is a person unworthy and unprepared?

A person is unworthy and unprepared when he or she does not believe or doubts Christ's words, since the words "for you" require all hearts to believe.

303. How are we to examine ourselves before receiving the Sacrament?

We are to examine ourselves to see whether

A. we are sorry for our sins;

959 **Ps. 38:18** I confess my iniquity; I am troubled by my sin.

960 **2 Cor. 7:10–11** Godly sorrow brings repentance that leads to salvation and leaves no regret, but worldly sorrow brings death. See what this godly sorrow has produced in you.

B. we believe in our Savior Jesus Christ and in His words in the Sacrament;

961 **Luke 22:19–20** This is My body given for you. . . . This cup is the new covenant in My blood, which is poured out for you.

962 **2 Cor. 13:5** Examine yourselves to see whether you are in the faith; test yourselves.

C. we plan, with the help of the Holy Spirit, to change our sinful lives.

963 **Eph. 4:22–24** Put off, concerning your former conduct, the old man which grows corrupt accord-

ing to the deceitful lusts, and be renewed in the spirit of your mind, and . . . put on the new man which was created according to God, in righteousness and true holiness (NKJV).

As a preparation for the Sacrament, use "Christian Questions with Their Answers."

304. May those who are weak in faith come to the Lord's Table?

Yes, for Christ instituted the Sacrament for the very purpose of strengthening and increasing our faith.

964   **Mark 9:24** I do believe; help me overcome my unbelief.

965   **John 6:37** Whoever comes to Me I will never drive away.

305. Who must not be given the Sacrament?

The Sacrament must not be given to the following:

A. Those who are openly ungodly and unrepentant, including those who take part in non-Christian religious worship.

966   **1 Cor. 5:11, 13** You must not associate with anyone who calls himself a brother but is sexually immoral or greedy, an idolater or a slanderer, a drunkard or a swindler. With such a man do not even eat. . . . "Expel the wicked man from among you."

967   **1 Cor. 10:20–21** The sacrifices of pagans are offered to demons, not to God, and I do not want you to be participants with demons. You cannot drink the cup of the Lord and the cup of demons too; you cannot have a part in both the Lord's table and the table of demons.

B. Those who are unforgiving, refusing to be reconciled. They show thereby that they do not really believe that God forgives them either.

968   **Matt. 6:15** If you do not forgive men their sins, your Father will not forgive your sins.

Bible narrative: The unmerciful servant **(Matt. 18: 21–35).**

C. Those of a different confession of faith, since the Lord's Supper is a testimony of the unity of faith.

969   **Acts 2:42** They devoted themselves to the apostles' teaching and to the fellowship, to the breaking of bread and to prayer.

970   **1 Cor. 10:17** Because there is one loaf, we, who are many, are one body, for we all partake of the one loaf.

971   **1 Cor. 11:26** Whenever you eat this bread and drink this cup, you proclaim the Lord's death until He comes.

972   **Rom. 16:17** Watch out for those who cause divisions and put obstacles in your way that are contrary to the teaching you have learned. Keep away from them.

D. Those who are unable to examine themselves, such as infants, people who have not received proper instruction, or the unconscious.

973   **1 Cor. 11:28** A man ought to examine himself before he eats of the bread and drinks of the cup.

Note: Pastors as stewards of the mysteries of God **(1 Cor. 4:1)** have the greatest responsibility as to who should be admitted to the Sacrament. Some of the responsibility also rests with the congregation and the communicant.

306. What is confirmation?

Confirmation is a public rite of the church preceded by a period of instruction designed to help baptized Christians identify with the life and mission of the Christian community.

Note: Prior to admission to the Lord's Supper, it is necessary to be instructed in the Christian faith **(1 Cor. 11:28).** The rite of confirmation provides an opportunity for the individual Christian, relying on God's promise given in Holy Baptism, to make a personal public confession of the faith and a lifelong pledge of fidelity to Christ.

974   **Matt. 10:32–33** Whoever acknowledges Me before men, I will also acknowledge him before My Father in heaven. But whoever disowns Me before men, I will disown him before My Father in heaven.

975   **Rev. 2:10** Be faithful, even to the point of death, and I will give you the crown of life.

APPENDIX

Luther's Preface

[Luther included this preface to the Small Catechism which addresses particular issues of his day.]

Martin Luther, to all faithful and godly pastors and preachers: grace, mercy, and peace be yours in Jesus Christ, our Lord.

The deplorable, miserable conditions which I recently observed when visiting the parishes have constrained and pressed me to put this catechism of Christian doctrine into this brief, plain, and simple form. How pitiable, so help me God, were the things I saw: the common man, especially in the villages, knows practically nothing of Christian doctrine, and many of the pastors are almost entirely incompetent and unable to teach. Yet all the people are supposed to be Christians, have been baptized, and receive the Holy Sacrament even though they do not know the Lord's Prayer, the Creed, or the Ten Commandments and live like poor animals of the barnyard and pigpen. What these people have mastered, however, is the fine art of tearing all Christian liberty to shreds.

Oh, you bishops! How will you ever answer to Christ for letting the people carry on so disgracefully and not attending to the duties of your office even for a moment? One can only hope judgment does not strike you! You command the Sacrament in one kind only, insist on the observance of your human ways, and yet are unconcerned whether the people know the Lord's Prayer, the Creed, the Ten Commandments, or indeed any of God's Word. Woe, woe to you forever!

Therefore dear brothers, for God's sake I beg all of you who are pastors and preachers to devote yourselves sincerely to the duties of your office, that you feel compassion for the people entrusted to your care, and that you help us accordingly to inculcate this catechism in the people, especially the young. If you cannot do more, at least take the tables and charts for catechism instruction and drill the people in them word for word, in the following way:

First, the pastor should most carefully avoid teaching the Ten Commandments, the Lord's Prayer, the Creed, the sacraments, etc., according to various texts and differing forms. Let him adopt one version, stay with it, and from one year to the next keep using it unchanged. Young and inexperienced persons must be taught a single fixed form or they will easily become confused, and the result will be that all previous effort and labor will be lost. There should be no change, even though one may wish to improve the text.

The honored fathers understood this well, and therefore they all consistently used one form of the Lord's Prayer, the Creed, and the Ten Commandments. We should do as they did by teaching these materials to the young and the common man without altering a single syllable and by never varying their wording when presenting or quoting them year after year.

So adopt whatever form you wish, and then stick with it at all times. If, however, you happen to be preaching to some sophisticated, learned audience, then you certainly may demonstrate your skill with words by turning phrases as colorfully and masterfully as you can. But with young persons keep to a single, fixed, and permanent form and wording, and teach them first of all the Ten Commandments, the Creed, the Lord's Prayer, etc., according to the text, word for word, so that they can repeat it after you and commit it to memory.

But those who refuse to learn are to be told that they are denying Christ and do not belong to Him. They are not to be admitted to the Sacrament, accepted as sponsors at Baptism, or allowed to exercise Christian liberty in any way. They should instead be simply directed back to the pope and his functionaries, yes, even to Satan himself. Moreover, their parents and superiors should refuse them food and drink, telling them that the prince is of a mind to expel such rude persons from his realm, and so on.

Of course we cannot, and we should not try to, force the Christian faith on anyone. Yet we should steadily keep on urging people toward it and help them know what is considered right and wrong in the society in which they want to live and earn their living. A person who wants to live in a certain city and enjoy its privileges should know and observe its laws, no matter whether he believes in them or is at heart a rogue or scoundrel.

Second, after they have well memorized the text (of the catechism), then explain the meaning so that they understand what they are saying. Do so again with the help of these charts or some other brief uniform method of your choosing; adhere to it and do not change a single syllable, as said above concerning the text, taking your time with it. For it is not necessary to teach everything at once, but one thing after the other. After they understand well the meaning of the First Commandment, proceed to the Second, and so on, otherwise they will be too overwhelmed to the point of remembering nothing.

Third, after you have so taught them this short catechism, take up the Large Catechism and use it to give them a broader and richer understanding. Here enlarge on every individual commandment, petition, segment, explaining in each case the various words, uses, benefits, dangers, and hurts involved, as you will find them amply described in many a book dealing with these topics. Stress especially that commandment or any other specific part of the catechism doctrine which your people neglect most. For example, among craftsmen and merchants, farmers and employees, you must powerfully stress the Seventh Commandment, which forbids stealing, because among such people many kinds of dishonesty and thievery occur. Also, for young persons and the common man you must stress the Fourth Commandment, urging them to be orderly, faithful, obedient, and peaceable, always bringing in many Bible examples of how God punished or blessed such people.

You should particularly urge those in authority and parents to govern the young well and to send them to school. Show them why it is their duty to do this and explain what a damnable sin it is if they fail to do so. For by such neglect they ruin and destroy both the kingdom of God and that of this world and prove themselves to be the worst enemies of both God and man. Thoroughly underscore what terrible harm they do by not helping train children to become pastors, preachers, writers, and the like, and how God will punish them for it. There is a great need to preach about these things. For parents and those in authority are guilty beyond words in this regard, and the devil has horrible things in mind.

Finally, now that the pope's tyranny is over, people no longer want to go to the Sacrament but despise it. Here again urging is necessary, however, with the understanding that we are not to force anyone into the faith or to the Sacrament, nor set any law, time, or place for it. Our preaching should instead be such that of their own accord and without our command, people feel constrained themselves and press us pastors to serve the Sacrament. The way to go about this is to tell them that if anyone does not seek or desire the Lord's Supper at the very least four times a year, it is to be feared that he despises the Sacrament and is not Christian, just as no one is a Christian who does not believe or hear the Gospel. For Christ did not say, "Omit this" or "despise this," but "This do, as often as you drink it," etc. He most certainly wants it done and does not want it left undone and despised. "This do," He says.

For a person not to prize highly the Sacrament is tantamount to saying that he has no sin, no flesh, no devil, no world, no death, no danger, no hell. That is to say, he believes in none of these although he is over-whelmed by them and is the devil's possession twice over. On the other hand, he needs no grace, life, para-dise, kingdom of heaven, Christ, God, or any good thing. Surely, if he recognized how much evil is in him and how much he needs all the good things he lacks, he would not neglect the Sacrament, which gives help against such evil and bestows so much goodness. He will not need to be forced by law to the Sacrament but will himself come running in a hurry to the Lord's Table, constrained within himself and pressing you to give him the Sacrament.

Therefore do not set up any law concerning it, as the pope does. Only emphasize clearly the benefit, need, usefulness, and blessing connected with the Sacrament, and also the harm and danger of neglecting it. The people will then come of themselves without your using compulsion. But if they still do not come, then let them go their way and tell them that all who are insensitive or unaware of their great need and God's gracious help belong to the devil. But if you fail to urge these things or if you make it into law and bitterness, then the fault will be yours if they despise the Sacrament. Why should they not be lazy if you are asleep and silent?

So look to it, you pastors and preachers. Our ministry today is something else than it was under the pope. It has become a serious and saving responsibility. Consequently it now involves much more trouble and labor, danger and trial, and in addition it brings you little of the world's gratitude and rewards. But Christ Himself will be our reward if we labor faithfully. The Father of all grace help us to do just that. To Him be praise and thanks forever through Christ our Lord. Amen.

Books of the Bible

The Bible is divided into two parts, the Old Testament and the New Testament. There are 66 books in the Bible: 39 in the Old Testament and 27 in the New Testament.

Books of the Old Testament

Historical Books

The Pen´ ta-teuch
(Five Books of Moses)

Gen´ e-sis
Ex´ o-dus
Le-vit´ i-cus
Num´ bers
Deu-ter-on´ o-my

Other Historical Books

Josh´ u-a
Judg´es
Ruth
1 Sam´ u-el
2 Sam´ u-el
1 Kings
2 Kings
1 Chron´ i-cles
2 Chron´ i-cles
Ez´ ra
Ne-he-mi´ ah
Esther

Poetic Books

Job
Psalms
Proverbs
Ec-cle-si-as´ tes
Song of Songs

Prophetic Books

Major Prophets

I-sa´ iah
Jer-e-mi´ ah
Lam-en-ta´ tions
E-ze´ kiel
Dan´ iel

Minor Prophets

Ho-se´ a
Jo´ el
A´ mos
O-ba-di´ ah
Jo´ nah
Mi´ cah
Na´ hum
Hab-ak´ kuk
Zeph-a-ni´ ah
Hag´ gai
Zech-a-ri´ ah
Mal´ a-chi

Books of the New Testament

Historical Books

Mat´ thew

Mark

Luke

John

Acts

Epistles

Ro´ mans

1 Co-rin´ thi-ans

2 Co-rin´ thi-ans

Ga-la´ tians

E-phe´ sians

Phi-lip´ pi-ans

Co-los´ sians

1 Thes-sa-lo´ nians

2 Thes-sa-lo´ nians

1 Tim´ o-thy

2 Tim´ o-thy

Ti´ tus

Phi-le´ mon

He´ brews

James

1 Pe´ ter

2 Pe´ ter

1 John

2 John

3 John

Jude

Prophetic Book

Rev-e-la´ tion

Creeds and Confessions

In addition to the Apostles' Creed, the Nicene Creed, which is confessed at celebrations of the Lord's Supper, and the Athanasian Creed, often read on Holy Trinity Sunday, are universal statements of faith held by the Lutheran Church. Both concentrate especially on the person and work of Jesus Christ.

The Lutheran Church also accepts without reservation all the documents contained in The Book of Concord of 1580 as a true and unadulterated statement and exposition of the Word of God. The best known and most widely used of these is Dr. Martin Luther's Small Catechism.

Born Nov. 10, 1483, in Eisleben, Germany, Luther attended the University of Erfurt, regarded as the best of schools particularly in law and liberal arts. Soon after, however, he requested to be admitted to the Augustinian order. In 1507 he was consecrated a priest and later obtained a doctorate in theology. His break with the Roman Catholic Church in 1521 occurred after he was told to recant what he believed to be Scriptural teachings contrary to those of the Roman Church.

Luther's Small Catechism and his Large Catechism, completed in 1529, were originally intended to be helpful manuals for pastors and family heads in teaching God's Word to children and adults. The Large Catechism is not made up of questions and answers but presents basic Christian teachings in a form often used in sermons.

Another well-known statement of faith, the Augsburg Confession, was written by Philip Melanchthon and read before Emperor Charles V at Augsburg, Germany, in 1530. While friendly in tone, it was adopted as a testimony against abuses prevalent in the church and against the errors of certain reformers regarding such crucial doctrines as original sin and the sacraments.

In 1531 Melanchthon wrote the Apology (Defense) of the Augsburg Confession. It too became an official confession of faith among Lutherans by its adoption at Smalcald, Germany, in 1537. In great detail it answers criticisms of the Augsburg Confession. Virtually half of the Apology is devoted to the Biblical doctrine of justification by grace through faith in Jesus Christ.

The Smalcald Articles were written by Luther in 1536 and signed by many clergy present at Smalcald in 1537. The Articles are a summary of Luther's main disagreements with the Roman Church. Melanchthon's Treatise on the Power and Primacy of the Pope was also officially adopted at Smalcald.

The Formula of Concord, completed in 1577, served to resolve doctrinal differences among Lutherans and was approved by over 8,000 theologians, pastors, and teachers by 1580. It was not a new confession but an exposition and defense of the previously adopted writings.

Quotations from these writings are included in this explanation of the Small Catechism.

Explanation of Luther's Seal

Martin Luther designed the following seal
to summarize his Christian faith.

The black cross in the center reminds us that Jesus died to take the punishment for our sins. The red heart reminds us of the love God has for us in sending Jesus to be our Savior. The red of the heart is the color of the blood of Christ, shed for us and for our salvation. The white rose helps us remember the work of the Holy Spirit who makes us pure and holy in God's sight by bringing us to faith in Jesus and by helping us to live our lives for Him. The sky blue background pictures the joy of the new life God gives to all who believe and trust in Him. Finally, the golden ring outlining the seal reminds us of our eternal inheritance—a home in heaven where we will enjoy complete joy and happiness in our Savior's presence.

Salvation Outline

The following seven points summarize basic information about the human condition and God's saving grace. You may want to memorize these points so that you may share them with someone who does not yet believe in Jesus as his or her Savior.

1. *God loves you!* "For God so loved the world that He gave His one and only Son, that whoever believes in Him shall not perish but have eternal life" **(John 3:16).**

2. *You are a sinner.* "For all have sinned and fall short of the glory of God" **(Romans 3:23).**

3. *God punishes sin.* "For the wages of sin is death, but the gift of God is eternal life in Christ Jesus our Lord" **(Romans 6:23).**

4. *Jesus took our punishment.* "But God demonstrates His own love for us in this: While we were still sinners, Christ died for us" **(Romans 5:8).**

5. *Jesus rose from the dead.* "For what I received I passed on to you as of first importance: that Christ died for our sins according to the Scriptures, that He was buried, that He was raised on the third day according to the Scriptures" **(1 Corinthians 15:3–4).**

6. *Jesus offers forgiveness of sins and eternal life to those who believe in Him.* "He then brought them out and asked, 'Sirs, what must I do to be saved?' They replied, 'Believe in the Lord Jesus, and you will be saved—you and your household'" **(Acts 16:30–31).**

7. *Salvation is free—a gift from God.* "For it is by grace you have been saved, through faith—and this is not from yourselves, it is the gift of God—not by works, so that no one can boast" **(Ephesians 2:8–9).**

The Church Year

God's people use the Church Year calendar to help them in their worship life. The Church Year calendar has two halves. The festival half, extending from Advent through the Day of Pentecost, centers on the life of Christ, reminding us of what God has done and continues to do for us through His Son. The non-festival half, extending from Trinity Sunday through the Last Sunday of the Church Year, focuses on the life of the Church as it is strengthened daily by God's Word.

In all, there are six seasons of the Church Year: Advent, Christmas, Epiphany, Lent, Easter, and the Season after Pentecost. The following colors are associated with these seasons.

Blue: (Advent) reminds us of the blessed eternal hope that is ours in Christ.

White: (Christmas and Easter) is the color of purity, holiness, glory, and joy.

Green: (Epiphany and the Sundays after Pentecost/ Trinity) represents the Christian life and growth in the faith.

Purple: (Lent) reminds us of our need for repentance and preparation for the celebration of Easter.

Red: (Pentecost) the color of fire, representing the coming of the Holy Spirit; also used on certain saints' days to represent the blood of martyrs.

Contained within the Church Year are the feast days of Christmas, Epiphany, Easter, Ascension, and Pentecost. These days celebrate important events in the life of Christ and what they mean for us today. Other festivals are included on the Church Year chart.

The Church Year and Its Festivals

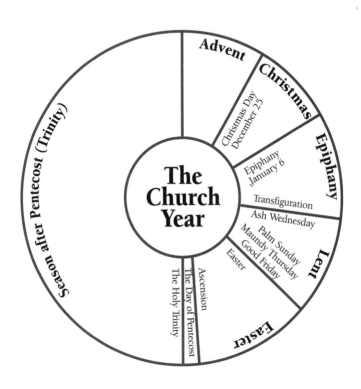

The Church Year

Sundays and Seasons

The Time of Christmas

Advent Season
First Sunday in Advent
Second Sunday in Advent
Third Sunday in Advent
Fourth Sunday in Advent

Christmas Season
The Nativity of Our Lord
    Christmas Eve
    Christmas Midnight
    Christmas Dawn
    Christmas Day
First Sunday after Christmas
Second Sunday after Christmas

Epiphany Season
The Epiphany of Our Lord
First Sunday after the Epiphany
    The Baptism of Our Lord
Second Sunday after the Epiphany
Third Sunday after the Epiphany
Fourth Sunday after the Epiphany
Fifth Sunday after the Epiphany
Sixth Sunday after the Epiphany
Seventh Sunday after the Epiphany   *Three-Year Lectionary*
Eighth Sunday after the Epiphany
Last Sunday after the Epiphany
    The Transfiguration of Our Lord

The Time of Easter

Pre-Lent Season
Septuagesima
Sexagesima   *One-Year Lectionary*
Quinquagesima

Lenten Season
Ash Wednesday
First Sunday in Lent
Second Sunday in Lent
Third Sunday in Lent
Fourth Sunday in Lent
Fifth Sunday in Lent

Holy Week
Palm Sunday
    Sunday of the Passion
Monday in Holy Week
Tuesday in Holy Week
Wednesday in Holy Week
Holy Thursday
Good Friday

Easter Season
The Resurrection of Our Lord
    Easter Vigil   Easter Evening/Monday
    Easter Sunrise   Easter Tuesday
    Easter Day   Easter Wednesday
Second Sunday of Easter
Third Sunday of Easter
Fourth Sunday of Easter
Fifth Sunday of Easter
Sixth Sunday of Easter
The Ascension of Our Lord
Seventh Sunday of Easter

Pentecost
    Pentecost Eve   Pentecost Evening/Monday
    Day of Pentecost   Pentecost Tuesday

The Time of the Church

The Season after Pentecost
The Holy Trinity
Second through Twenty-seventh Sunday
    after Pentecost *(Three-Year Lectionary)*
First through Twenty-sixth Sunday after
    Trinity *(One-Year Lectionary)*
Last Sunday of the Church Year

Feasts and Festivals

November
30 St. Andrew, Apostle

December
21 St. Thomas, Apostle
26 St. Stephen, Martyr
27 St. John, Apostle and Evangelist
28 The Holy Innocents, Martyrs
31 Eve of the Circumcision and Name of Jesus

January
 1 Circumcision and Name of Jesus
18 The Confession of St. Peter
24 St. Timothy, Pastor and Confessor
25 The Conversion of St. Paul
26 St. Titus, Pastor and Confessor

February
 2 The Purification of Mary and the
   Presentation of Our Lord
24 St. Matthias, Apostle

March
19 St. Joseph, Guardian of Jesus
25 The Annunciation of Our Lord

April
25 St. Mark, Evangelist

May
1 St. Philip and St. James, Apostles
31 The Visitation *(Three-Year Lectionary)*

June
11 St. Barnabas, Apostle
24 The Nativity of St. John the Baptist
29 St. Peter and St. Paul, Apostles

July
2 The Visitation *(One-Year Lectionary)*
22 St. Mary Magdalene
25 St. James the Elder, Apostle

August
15 St. Mary, Mother of Our Lord
24 St. Bartholomew, Apostle
29 The Martyrdom of St. John the Baptist

September
14 Holy Cross Day
21 St. Matthew, Apostle and Evangelist
29 St. Michael and All Angels

October
18 St. Luke, Evangelist
23 St. James of Jerusalem, Brother of Jesus and Martyr
28 St. Simon and St. Jude, Apostles
31 Reformation Day

November
1 All Saints' Day

Terms Relating to Worship and God's House

Acolyte. Person who lights and extinguishes the candles at church services.

Agnus Dei. Latin for "Lamb of God." See **John 1:29.**

Alleluia. Hebrew word meaning "praise the LORD."

Altar. A stone or wooden structure at the center of the chancel from which the Lord's Supper is celebrated. Altars remind us of Christ's sacrifice on the cross for us.

Antiphon. A verse of Scripture repeated at the beginning and ending of a psalm or Introit.

Benediction. A blessing from the Lord, spoken by the pastor at the conclusion of the service.

Benedictus. Latin for "blessed." Song of Zecharaiah **(Luke 1:68–79)** sung as the canticle in Matins.

Canticle. Sung liturgical text, usually drawn from the Bible (for example, the Magnificat and Benedictus).

Celebrant. The pastor presiding at the celebration of the Lord's Supper.

Chancel. Front of the church containing the altar and pulpit. Area of the church from which the service is led.

Collect. A brief, structured prayer.

Compline. Service of prayer at the close of the day.

Crucifix. A cross bearing the image of the crucified Savior. The crucifix reminds us of Christ's sacrifice for us.

Divine Service. The name for the regular, weekly service that includes the celebration of the Lord's Supper.

Doxology. Words of praise addressed to the triune God.

Epistle. From the Greek word for "letter." In the Divine Service, the Epistle is the second reading, usually drawn from an Epistle in the New Testament (see p. 254).

Gloria in Excelsis. Latin meaning "glory in the highest." A Hymn of Praise in the Divine Service.

Gloria Patri. Latin for "glory to the Father." A liturgical text used to conclude a psalm or Introit.

Gradual. A liturgical response, drawn from the Bible, which follows the Old Testament Reading.

Holy Week. The week before Easter, which includes Palm Sunday, Maundy Thursday, and Good Friday.

Hosanna. Hebrew word of praise meaning "Save us now." Included in the Sanctus.

Hymn. A song of prayer or praise in stanza form.

Introit. From the Latin for "enter." Psalm verses sung or spoken at the beginning of the Divine Service.

Invocation. From the Latin "to call upon." The words "In the name of the Father and of the Son and of the Holy Spirit" spoken at the beginning of the service.

Kyrie eleison. Greek for "Lord, have mercy."

Lectern. A stand with a bookrest from which the Scriptures are read.

Lectionary. Book or list of appointed Scripture readings for the Sundays and festivals of the Church Year.

Litany. A structured form of prayer consisting of a series of petitions and responses.

Liturgy. Greek word meaning "public service." See also Divine Service.

Magnificat. Latin for "magnify, praise" from the Song of Mary **(Luke 1:46–55).**

Matins. Morning service of psalms, readings, and prayers.

Maundy Thursday. Also called Holy Thursday, the day when Jesus instituted the Lord's Supper. *Maundy* is from the Latin for "command," referring to the new command Jesus gave to "love one another" **(John 13:34).**

Narthex. Hall or room at the entrance to the church.

Nave. From the Latin word for "ship." The main part of the church where the congregation assembles for worship.

Nunc Dimittis. Latin for "now [let your servant] depart," from the Song of Simeon **(Luke 2:29–32).**

Offertory. Biblical text usually sung as the offering is received at the altar.

Ordinary. Parts of the service that remain the same from week to week, for example the Kyrie and Sanctus.

Funeral Pall. Large white cloth that covers the casket, reminding us that we are clothed in Christ's righteousness through Baptism **(Galatians 3:27).**

Paraments. Cloths placed on the altar, pulpit, and lectern in the color of the season of the Church Year.

Pax Domini. Latin for "peace of the Lord."

Pericope. Greek word meaning "a section." Portions of Holy Scripture read on a given Sunday.

Propers. Parts of the service that change from week to week, for example the Introit and Scripture readings.

Preface. Responses at the beginning of the Service of the Sacrament, followed by the Proper Preface, which changes seasonally.

Pulpit. A raised platform or stand from which the pastor preaches the sermon.

Responsory. Scripture verses sung or spoken after the reading of Scripture in Matins, Vespers, and Compline.

Salutation. "The Lord be with you," followed by the response "And also with you" or "And with your Spirit."

Sanctus. Latin for "holy." Follows the Preface in the Service of the Sacrament. Based on **Isaiah 6:3** and **Matthew 21:9.**

Stanza. A numbered division within a hymn.

Te Deum. Latin for "[We praise] You, O God." Ancient Hymn of Praise sung in Matins.

Venite. Latin for "O come." Initial words of Psalm 95, sung as the first psalm in Matins.

Verse. Portions of Scripture sung or spoken immediately before the Holy Gospel in the Divine Service.

Vespers. Evening service of psalms, readings, and prayers.

Vestments. Liturgical garments worn by the pastor, acolytes, choir, and others assisting in worship.

Words of Our Lord. The words of Jesus spoken by the pastor over the bread and wine in the Service of the Sacrament. Also known as the Words of Institution.

The Time between the Testaments (432–5 BC)

During the years between the end of the events of the Old Testament and the beginning of the New Testament, God was preparing the world, and His people in particular, for the coming of the Savior. And then, "when the time had fully come, God sent His Son, born of a woman, born under law, to redeem those under law, that we might receive the full rights of sons **(Galatians 4:4).**

What political forces bridged the testaments as God set the world's stage for the coming of Jesus?

- *The Diaspora* (Dispersion) Jewish people scattered throughout the world as the result of the Babylonian captivity. The Jews that assembled in Jerusalem to hear Peter's Pentecost sermon had come there from all over the world. Early Christians began their mission efforts among these transplanted Jews who were familiar with the Greek translation of the Old Testament.

- *Persian Period* (430–332 BC) Beginning with King Cyrus's decree in 538 BC, many of God's people began returning to the Promised Land. But their homeland remained a minor entity held under the control of a number of significant political powers, beginning with Persians. Life under the Persians was for the most part tolerant. (Esther had been a queen of Persia.)

- *Greek Period* (332–167 BC) The conquest of Palestine by young Alexander the Great in 332 BC began a period of Greek cultural influence. Greek could be heard spoken throughout the world.

During this period the Old Testament was translated into Greek (called the Septuagint). Following Alexander's death, the empire was divided among his generals. Palestine was passed back and forth from the governance of the Seleucids and the Ptolemies. The Jews enjoyed good treatment under the Ptolemies, but things were different under Seleucid Antiochus Epiphanes who ruled from 175–164 BC. He hated the Jews and sought to wipe out them and their religion. He attacked Jerusalem, defiled the temple, placed a sow on the Jewish altar, erected a statue of Jupiter, prohibited worship and circumcision, sold Jewish families into slavery, and destroyed every copy of Scripture he could find.

- *Hasmonean Period* (167–63 BC) In opposition to the atrocities of Antiochus, the head of a priestly family, Mattathias, and his five sons led a successful revolt and founded a dynasty that, unfortunately, all too soon resembled that of the Seleucids.

- *Roman Period* (63 BC to the time of Christ) In 63 BC, Romans conquered Jerusalem. They killed the priest serving at the temple and defiled the Most Holy Place. Antipater (a descendent of Esau) was appointed the ruler of Judea. His son, Herod the Great, rebuilt the temple in an attempt to earn favor with the Jews. But Herod was cruel and insecure. He was the ruler when Jesus was born, and he ordered the killing of the children of Bethlehem.

What Holy Scriptures and other writings were God's people reading during this period?

- The Septuagint—according to tradition, this translation of the books of the Old Testament from Hebrew into Greek was made in Alexandria, Egypt, at the request of Ptolemy Philadephus (285–247 BC). Septuagint comes from the Latin word for seventy. According to Jewish tradition, seventy-two scholars did the work in seventy-two days, translating the entirety of the Old Testament canon. The Septuagint was commonly used during the time of Christ and in the Early Christian Church as it was written in Greek, a language understood by Jews and Gentiles alike. The Septuagint is frequently quoted in the New Testament by Jesus and the apostles.

- The Apocrypha—identifies fourteen books positioned between the Old and New Testaments of some Bibles. Written between the first and third centuries BC, these books are not found in the Hebrew Old Testament and were never quoted by Jesus. The Apocrypha, a name derived from a Greek word meaning "hidden," includes 1 Esdras, 2 Esdras, Tobit, Judith, Rest of Esther, Wisdom of Solomon, Ecclesiasticus, Baruch, Song of the Three Holy Children, History of Susanna, Bel and the Dragon, Prayer of Manasses, 1 Maccabees, and 2 Maccabees.

What language did people speak in the Holy Land when Jesus was born?

After the return of God's people from Babylonian Captivity, Aramaic gradually replaced Hebrew as the language commonly spoken by the people of Palestine. Aramaic was the ancient language of Syria and it is similar to Hebrew. Jesus spoke and taught in Aramaic, but He was undoubtedly also familiar with Hebrew, Greek, and perhaps Latin.

Who were the religious groups that figure prominently in the New Testament?

- Sanhedrin—thought to have originated in the third century BC, this group of seventy members led the Jewish people in the days of Christ. Among the seventy members were priests, Sadducees, Pharisees, scribes, and elders. The high priest presided over the group.

- Pharisees—a sect that rose as a reaction to those among God's people desiring to adopt Greek culture with its pagan religions. The Pharisees interpreted God's Law so the people could live righteously before God according to it. They wielded powerful influence among the people and were the only Jewish religious group to survive the destruction of the temple in AD 70. Modern Judaism can be traced to them.

- Sadducees—an aristocratic sect heavily influenced by secular thought and Greek customs, they were liberals and freethinkers. Though they controlled the Sanhedrin, they were appropriately characterized as irreligious in nature. Unlike the Pharisees, the Sadducees did not believe in the resurrection **(Mark 12:18).**

- Scribes—copied, studied, and interpreted Scripture. Because of their vast knowledge they were considered experts in the Law and sometimes served as lawyers. The role of scribes was especially important before the days of printing.

Where did the people worship in the New Testament world?

- The temple—the physical structure built as God's dwelling place among His people. Located in Jerusalem, the temple remained the center of Jewish worship. Here people came to offer blood sacrifices for the sins of the people and to pray. Jesus, the ultimate indwelling of God among His people, referred to Himself as a temple **(John 2:19–21).** He came to take away the sins of all people once and for all **(Hebrews 9:24–26).**

- Synagogues—houses for religious teaching and worship, synagogues were begun during the days of exile when the people were cut off from the temple. Early Christians modeled their church life and elements of worship after that of the synagogue.

- Homes—the Passover meal was a family event from the time of its first observance **(Exodus 12).** In Jewish tradition, the head of the household was responsible for the faith nurture and devotional life of the family. Similarly, this responsibility exists among Christian families **(Ephesians 6:4).** Luther noted this frequently in the catechism, summarizing Christian doctrine "as the head of the family should teach it in a simple way to his household." Early Christians, especially during times of persecution, met in small groups in people's homes to worship, support, and encourage one another, and to enjoy a time of fellowship.

What features made the world in which Christ was born ready to receive the world's Savior?

- Greek language gave the world a common voice. The Old Testament and eventually the New Testament languages were available in the universal language of the day.

- Roman transportation and communication facilitated the efficient spreading of the Gospel.

- The dispersion of God's people throughout the world provided strategic mission contacts so the message of salvation might be transmitted first to the Jews and then to the Gentiles.

- The promises of the Old Testament were ripe for fulfillment so that at just the right time and place Jesus, the stone the builders rejected, might give His life to save all people and in so doing construct a new religion of the old, "built on the foundation of the apostles and prophets, with Christ Jesus Himself as the chief cornerstone" **(Ephesians 2:20).**

Symbols and Their Meanings

Alpha and Omega, the first and last letters of the Greek alphabet, remind us of Jesus' words, "I am the Alpha and Omega, . . . who is, and who was, and who is to come, the Almighty" **(Revelation 1:8).**

Like an anchor keeps a ship safely in position, our hope in Christ keeps believers safe and secure **(Hebrews 6:19).**

Through the Sacrament of Baptism the Holy Spirit gives us God's gifts of faith, forgiveness, and salvation.

Through God's Word the Holy Spirit works faith, and through faith eternal life **(John 20:31).**

A caterpillar emerges from a cocoon as a beautiful and changed creature. This is a symbol of the resurrection from the dead **(1 Corinthians 15:51–54).**

Jesus is the light of the world **(John 8:12)**.

Our God is eternal, without beginning or end **(1 Timothy 1:17)**.

Our triune God is eternal, without a beginning or an ending **(Genesis 21:33; Acts 7:55)**.

Chi-Rho. This symbol is made up of the first two letters of the Greek word for Christ. The Greek word *Christ* means "Messiah" or "the Anointed." **(John 17:3)**.

Our God is triune, three persons in one Godhead—Father, Son, and Holy Spirit **(Matthew 3:16–17)**.

Jesus has won for us victory over death and an eternal home in heaven **(Revelation 2:10)**.

The Lord's Supper. Those participating in this Sacrament receive bread and wine together with the body and blood of Christ Jesus for the forgiveness of sins, new life, and eternal salvation **(Matthew 26:26–29; Mark 14:22–25; Luke 22:17–20; 1 Corinthians 11:23–25).**

God sees and knows all things **(Hebrews 4:13).**

Matthew—a winged man. His Gospel begins with a list of the ancestors of Jesus.

Mark—a winged lion. Mark's Gospel begins by describing the voice of one crying in the wilderness.

Luke—a winged ox. Luke provides the most detail of the sacrificial suffering and death of Christ.

John—an eagle. John's Gospel soars with Christ's love and power.

The seven-fold gifts of the Holy Spirit **(Isaiah 11:2–3).** The Holy Spirit gives us His gifts through the means of grace—God's Word and the Sacraments.

Symbol of the Holy Trinity **(Matthew 28:19).**

The Greek cross. Five Greek crosses, for the five wounds of Christ **(John 20:19–20),** are sometimes seen on altar cloths.

God the Father. The hand of creation and blessing **(Psalm 145:13–16).**

Latin cross. This favorite and most widely recognized of the crosses represents that upon which Jesus gave His life for the sins of the world **(Acts 2:23).**

Maltese cross. Each point on this cross represents one of the eight Beatitudes from Christ's Sermon on the Mount **(Matthew 5:3–10).**

Tau cross. This cross (also called the Old Testament cross or the cross of prophecy, shaped for the cross Moses raised in the wilderness) connects Old Testament prophecy with the fulfillment of the promise of salvation in Christ Jesus **(John 3:14–15).**

Prayer. Rising smoke reminds us of the prayers of God's people ascending to Him **(Revelation 8:4; Psalm 141:2).**

For us and for our salvation, our Savior suffered under Pontius Pilate **(John 19:1–3).**

The Holy Spirit. The Spirit of God descended like a dove upon Jesus at His Baptism.

The Lord's Supper. Through these commonly harvested elements of the earth, bread and wine are made. In the Lord's Supper participants receive Christ's very body and blood together with bread and wine for the forgiveness of sins, new life, and eternal salvation **(Matthew 26:26–29; Mark 14:22–25; Luke 22:17–20, 1 Corinthians 11:23–25).**

This symbol is the first three letters of the Greek word for Jesus. The name *Jesus* means "the Lord saves" **(Matthew 1:21).**

This is the abbreviation of the inscription Pilate had fastened to Jesus' cross reading, "Jesus of Nazareth, the King of the Jews" **(John 19:19)**.

Ichthus is the Greek word for fish. Each letter of this word is also regarded as an acronym for the words "Jesus Christ, God's Son, Savior" **(1 John 1:7)**. The word for fish and the fish itself became symbols of early Christians.

Our Lord's gift of the keys of the kingdom, the power of the Church to forgive and retain sins **(Matthew 16: 18–19)**.

Agnus Dei. Jesus is the Lamb of God who takes away the sins of the world **(Isaiah 53:7; John 1:29; Revelation 5:12)**.

The Word of God. God directs and enlightens God's people **(Psalm 119:115)**.

God's plan is for husbands and wives to love each other and to live for Him in marriage, just as Christ loved the Church and gave Himself up for the Church to make it holy **(Ephesians 5:25–31)**.

Jesus was nailed to the cross to suffer and die for our sins **(John 20:25)**.

Like a fisherman who gathers fish in a net and then sorts them, at the end of time the angels will separate believers from unbelievers **(Matthew 13:47–49)**. The net represents the Church and the kingdom of heaven.

Palm branches remind us of the victory that is ours in Jesus **(Revelation 7:9–10)**.

Prayer. God commands and invites believers in Jesus Christ to pray and promises to hear and answer us **(1 Thessalonians 5:16–18)**.

Christ is our rock, the foundation upon which we build our lives **(1 Corinthians 10:4).**

Christmas rose. Symbol of the fulfillment of the Messianic prophecy **(Song of Songs 2:1).**

Baptism. Three drops of water remind us of the triune God in whose name we are baptized **(Matthew 28:19).**

The Church. Just as God saved Noah and his family in the ark, God saves His people through the faith He imparts through the means of grace, His gifts to the Church **(1 Peter 3:18–21).**

Star representing the six days of creation **(Genesis 1:16).** This six-pointed star is known to the Jews as the star of David.

Spiritus Gladius. The sword of the Spirit is the Word of God **(Ephesians 6:17).** *Spiritus Gladius* means "spirit sword" in Latin.

"I am the good shepherd," said Jesus **(John 10:11).** Jesus cares and provides for us; He laid down His life to save us.

God's Law tells us what we are to do and not to do and how to act. No one can keep God's Law. Jesus kept the Law in our place and without sin **(Hebrews 4:15).**

Christians let their light shine as they share the Good News of salvation through Jesus **(Matthew 5:16).**

The triangle has three sides. It reminds us of the one true God—Father, Son, and Holy Spirit **(Matthew 28:19).**

"I am the true vine," said Jesus **(John 15:1).** Jesus nourishes and sustains His people through the means of grace.

Index of Biblical Quotations

References are to question numbers in the explanation of the Small Catechism.

Index of Topics

References are to question numbers in the explanation of the Small Catechism.

Library of Congress Cataloging-in-Publication Data

Luther, Martin, 1483–1546
   [Kleine Katechismus. English]
   Luther's small catechism with explanation / Martin Luther.
   Translation of: Kleine Katechismus.
   Summary: Contains the basic principles of the Lutheran religion with some
explanation.
     ISBN 13: 978-0-7586-1121-5
     ISBN 10:   0-7586-1121-8
   1. Lutheran Church—Catechisms—English—Juvenile literature. 2. Catechisms,
English—Juvenile literature. [1. Lutheran Church—Catechisms. 2. Catechisms.]
I. Title.
BX8070.L72A4   1991
238´.41—dc20   90-45511
                                           CIP
                                           AC

ISBN 13: 978-0-7586-1121-5
ISBN 10:   0-7586-1121-8

9 780758 611215

Theology & Doctrine
22-3079